Wicca Practical Magic

Wicca

PRACTICAL MAGIC

THE GUIDE TO GET STARTED WITH MAGICAL HERBS, OILS, AND CRYSTALS

Patti Wigington

FALL RIVER PRESS

New York

FALL RIVER PRESS

New York

An Imprint of Sterling Publishing Co., Inc.
1166 Avenue of the Americas
New York, NY 10036

Interior text © 2017 Patti Wigington
Cover photography © Shannon Douglas
Illustrations © Tom Bingham
Icon illustration © Megan Dailey

ISBN 978-1-4351-6754-4

For information about custom editions, special sales, and premium
and corporate purchases, please contact Sterling Special Sales at
800-805-5489 or specialsales@sterlingpublishing.com.

Manufactured in the United States of America

2 4 6 8 10 9 7 5 3 1

sterlingpublishing.com

Design by Annabelle Gould

For all my Stone Circle brothers and sisters,
who help to keep me grounded
when I need it the most.

CONTENTS

Introduction

As someone who began exploring modern Pagan beliefs—including but certainly not limited to Wicca—nearly 30 years ago, I've been fortunate enough to spend my entire adult life as part of the greater Pagan and Wiccan community. I've always been fascinated by history, religion, and mythology from around the world, and the first time I had a conversation with a practicing Wiccan, something suddenly clicked for me. It was as though all the things I'd spent my formative years reading about—prayers, rituals, ancient gods and goddesses—suddenly became real, and not just echoes of long-gone civilizations. The period since then has been a journey of growth and development, and I've had the opportunity to study with and learn from some incredibly wise people. Perhaps even more important, I've been able to take the information I've gathered and use it to help myself live magically every single day.

I work with the gods and goddesses of my tradition regularly. I pray to them daily, I make offerings at my household altar, and I call upon them for assistance when I think they may be able to help me. Sometimes, I just give them a shout-out to say hello or thank you. Certainly, over the past three decades, various deities have come and gone in my life periodically, but they've always made themselves known to me, and I always make a point of letting them know that their attention is appreciated. I utilize magical crystals, oils, and herbs, both in ritual and in practical spellwork applications. When I find myself stuck and in need of a bit of soul searching and self-awareness, prayer and meditation come as second nature. If I've got questions about *where* my life is going, *how best* to respond to various aspects of my world, or *why* I should make one choice versus another, a little bit of divination is a handy tool in the magical arsenal. Just like with any other endeavor, if you practice Wicca long enough, it becomes a habit.

I was raised by agnostic parents who always encouraged me to read widely and explore new things. As a young adult, I was drawn to Wicca; it was the next logical progression for me, since I had spent nearly all my childhood and teenage years with my nose buried in books about history, mythology, and folklore. Wicca, with its emphasis on magical thinking, nature, and duality, seemed like the perfect fit for me. In the years since then, I've figured out that I'm not the only one with this experience; many people who begin exploring Wicca describe their journey as one that feels very much like "coming home."

In 2007, I became the Paganism and Wicca expert for About.com. Since then, it's been my pleasure to draw on my own experiences and studies to share them with readers, and I'm grateful to have been blessed with the chance to encounter so many wonderful people in the Pagan community. From High Priestesses and Priests to educators and activists, they've shared their knowledge with me. They've taught me how to craft rituals and spells, read Tarot cards, and even lead a séance. They've shown me the value of weaving a community, treating the earth as a sacred place, and standing up for those who cannot stand up for themselves. I've learned something new almost every day during the nearly three decades I've studied Wicca and other forms of Paganism, and now I'm excited to share that information with you.

This book's primary focus is on the practical applications of Wicca. We'll talk a bit about the basics of what Wicca actually is, and you'll see how you can use magical herbs, crystals, oils, and more as part of your daily practice. In other words, you'll learn that all these different aspects of magical living can be incorporated into spellwork, ritual, and honoring the gods and goddesses each day. We'll spend some time talking about the gods/deities, divinatory objects, candles and color significance, and many of the other magical tools that make for an effective Wicca practice. Once you begin incorporating magic into your day-to-day life, you'll feel liberated and empowered, allowing you to evolve into the best version of you that you can possibly become.

PART I

Wiccan Foundations

"Take the time to stop and appreciate all that is about you. Smell the earth, the trees, the leaves. Absorb their energies and send them yours . . . Show your respect and love for nature and live with nature."

—Raymond Buckland, *Complete Book of Witchcraft*

Before we really get into the meat of how to practice Wiccan magic, it's important to understand the history behind the religious structure. Although witchcraft itself has been practiced for thousands of years, Wicca, by comparison, is very new—and we'll talk in chapter 1 about the differences between the two.

CHAPTER ONE
A Call to Nature

I n the 1930s, Gerald Gardner, a British civil servant, returned to his homeland after many years abroad in Madeira, Ceylon (Sri Lanka), and British Malaya (now part of Malaysia). During his travels, Gardner developed an appreciation for indigenous cultures and, in particular, native magic and ritual practice. Once back in England, he began exploring European occult beliefs and was eventually initiated into the New Forest coven of witches. Shortly after the end of World War II, Gardner took the teachings of the New Forest group and combined them with Kabbalah, European mysticism, ceremonial magic, and a number of other philosophies to create a formal, structured tradition. Appropriately, it was called Gardnerian Wicca.

Gardner's original system was initiatory and oath-bound—meaning members had to be initiated by a High Priest or Priestess, and teachings were kept secret. Over the years, splinter groups formed and new traditions evolved. Today, most of the people who identify as Wiccan are not part of the Gardnerian tradition; many people in the Pagan community consider this form of practice *neo*-Wicca. This doesn't mean it's inferior to the original system; it's simply different.

Regardless of how you practice, you'll find that there are several common threads throughout the various Wiccan paths. We'll start by exploring the principles that are nearly universal in Wiccan belief, as well as the differences between Wicca, witchcraft, and Paganism. We'll even look at some of the things that Wicca is not. Then, we'll get into the specifics to lay a foundation for solid practice—seasons and elements, the Sabbat and Esbat celebrations, and some basics of ritual for important times of your life.

> **"Magic is natural. It is a harmonious movement of energies to create needed change. If you wish to practice magic, all thoughts of it being paranormal or supernatural must be forgotten."**
>
> —Scott Cunningham, *Wicca: A Guide for the Solitary Practitioner*

Deep Roots

One of the most important aspects of modern Wiccan practice is a reverence for nature. There's a simple reason for this: The Divine is present in nature, so the natural world should be honored and respected as sacred. Because of this, Wiccan practice—and specifically, magic—typically involves utilizing elements directly from nature: herbs, stones, and other items.

This doesn't mean Wiccans *worship* stones and flowers and deer and birds, but it *does* mean that because nature is an extension of the Divine, these aspects of the natural world are viewed as sacred. In addition to veneration of nature, most Wiccans follow a polytheistic belief system, honoring both a god and goddess, or sometimes multiple deities. Unlike many mainstream religions, Wicca has a polarity in the Divine; masculine and feminine are considered equally powerful and valuable. Finally, Wiccans accept the existence of magic as part of the natural world. There's nothing supernatural about magic. It's a skill set that can be used either in tandem with the gods or separate from them, in order to manifest change in those things that cause us dissatisfaction.

Most Wiccans, although certainly not all, follow a few basic guidelines when it comes to magic, and the Wiccan Rede is perhaps the best known of these, offering a primary moral system for practicing Wiccans. Although the Rede is actually a fairly lengthy poem, the origins of which have been muddied over the years, people are most familiar with its final line: *An' it harm none, do what ye will.* The word *An'* is an archaic term for *if,* so many Wiccans interpret this to mean that magic—or non-magical behavior, for that matter—is fair game as long as it doesn't cause harm to other people. However, there is some fluidity to this, because while we can all objectively agree on the harmful nature of some actions, others are subjective. In most cases, you will be the only person who can decide how the Rede applies to your own sense of values, ethics, and morality.

In addition to the Rede, some Wiccans believe in the Threefold Law, or the Rule of Three. The Threefold Law is the acceptance that the energy your actions give to the universe and its inhabitants, good or bad, magically or otherwise, is visited back on you three times. Do good things, and you'll experience positive things in return. Act cruelly toward others, and people will treat you accordingly. Again, only you can decide if and how the Threefold Law applies within the framework of your beliefs.

Finally, a good deal of Wiccan ritual practice involves a reverence for the deities. Honoring the gods is an important aspect of magical living, from prayers to altars to rituals celebrating the power and energy of the Divine. In addition to honoring the gods, many Wiccans pay tribute to their ancestors on a regular basis. This helps us connect to those who came before us and allows them to live on in our memories.

Although understanding the basic tenets of Wicca is necessary for magical practice, it's equally necessary to be aware of what is not covered under those tenets. For while there are many things that Wicca *is*, there are certainly just as many things that Wicca *is not*.

Wicca vs. Witchcraft vs. Paganism: Not all witches are Wiccan, and not all Pagans are witches. *Paganism* is an umbrella term that covers a variety of nature-based and polytheistic religious systems. Wicca is a specific religion that falls under the heading of Paganism. Although some witches see witchcraft as their religion, for many people today, it is merely a set of practices and skills.

Wicca is not some new, weird cult—it's a legitimate religion, recognized as valid in the United States, Great Britain, and some Canadian provinces. It's practiced in even more places, including Australia, Germany, France, and many other countries. Wicca isn't—or at least, shouldn't be—something you do to shock your friends and family members. It isn't what you see on television or in the movies; Wiccan magic is not what's happening in *Charmed*, *The Craft*, or the Harry Potter series. After all, you're not going to learn to change your eye color with magic, levitate your friends, or disarm an opponent during a wizard's duel. Instead, Wiccan magic is used for healing, protection, prosperity, success, and transformation. Finally, Wicca is not a tool to be used to get back at your ex or workplace bullies, as it's certainly not a religion you should begin practicing out of anger.

Ultimately, people become Wiccan for a variety of reasons. Yours may not be the same reason as someone else's, and that's perfectly okay! Some people are drawn to Wicca because they are ready to embrace a polarity of masculine and feminine they find lacking in other faiths. Others explore Wiccan systems in search of self-empowerment or spiritual growth. Still others find that Wiccan ideals are in tune with what they already believe, and they had just never given it a name before. If you've been looking for a flexibility of belief and a lack of formalized doctrine, Wicca might just be what you're seeking.

The Modern Wiccan

When Gerald Gardner and his New Forest coven were practicing witchcraft in secret, they never would have imagined the resources that today's Wiccans have at their fingertips. As visibility increases, due in no small part to the technological advancements we've made, the Wiccan community is growing by leaps and bounds. In Gardner's era, early Wiccans were limited in practice and worship, by both geography and a practice of necessary secrecy.

The modern Wiccan has access to so much more information than our predecessors did, and we can expand our knowledge simply by tapping a keyboard or swiping our phone screen. Books about Wicca— from beginner level to more advanced—are available in bookstores by the hundreds, and metaphysical shops with an inventory of herbs and crystals exist in nearly every major metropolitan area and more than a few small towns.

As accessibility to information has grown, so has the Wiccan community, both in its number of individual, solitary practitioners, and in coven and group membership. If you've ever thought about practicing as part of a group, there are certainly advantages to joining a coven. Group practice often provides a structure or framework that you won't experience as a solitary practitioner, and working with other people does tend to allow for a sense of spiritual fellowship that is rare to the experience of practicing alone. On the other hand, solitary practitioners benefit because they don't have to coordinate schedules with a dozen other people, and there's no infighting over group responsibilities or privileges. In addition, if you're a solitary Wiccan, you're under no obligation to anyone but yourself and your deities.

If you've decided you'd like to explore practice with a coven or group, you may be wondering how to find other Wiccans. There are two absolutely invaluable resources: First, utilize the Internet. Meetup pages, Facebook groups, and Wiccan websites like Witchvox.com and Reddit.com/r/Wicca often present a chance to network and connect with Wiccans both online and in person. If you're in a city with a university campus, don't discount the use of college websites; many universities have student-run Pagan or Wiccan alliances that have strong online presences.

The second way to find other Wiccans might seem like an obvious one: Go where the Wiccans are. Find your local metaphysical bookstore or herb shop, or hang out in the New Age section at the library, and you're practically guaranteed to find like-minded individuals. Don't be shy; strike up a conversation and see where it takes you. At a minimum, you'll have a nice chat with a total stranger, and if you're lucky, you may just find someone who can guide you toward a greater network of Wiccans in your very own community.

Practical Magic

One of the things that Wiccans find the most empowering about their beliefs is the realization that anyone can make magic happen.

Deities

In traditional Wiccan practice, the Divine cosmic forces are known as the Lord and Lady, or the God and Goddess.

The Lady: The Lady is the Goddess, and represents the three stages of womanhood. She is often symbolized by the triple moon symbol, showing the waxing, full, and waning phases. These three phases represent the Goddess in her roles as the Maiden, the Mother, and the Crone, or wise old woman. The Maiden is youthful innocence and beauty, while the Mother is the creator of life. In her aspect as the Crone, the Lady is typically a symbol of sagacity, intuition, and knowledge, and she is usually pictured with water and cups.

The Lord: Sometimes referred to only as the God, the Lord is the embodiment of the sacred masculine. He is seen as the young and virile Horned God, associated with the fertility of spring. At different times of the year, he can be the Oak King or the Holly King, or even seen as the Sun God. He is associated with the sun itself, the fertility of the land, and with phallic symbols such as horns, antlers, branches, and wands.

The All: In some traditions of Wicca, there is another theological concept of the Divine known as the All or the One. This is an omnipotent and impersonal being that can never be truly known, only acknowledged. A pantheistic divinity, the All is found in every aspect of nature and is sometimes viewed as the life-creating force of the universe.

Manifesting magic is as simple as understanding our personal connections to the natural world, as well as to the gods and goddesses.

The herbs, oils, and crystals discussed in this book are part of the natural world, and each is representative of various properties called correspondences. Think of a correspondence as a signature or fingerprint; every natural item has them, and they are as varied as nature itself. By combining natural items, we can create unique blends of correspondences to suit just about any magical purpose we like. Whether we hope to obtain love or money, bring about healing or abundance, develop our intuition, or protect our family and home, nature provides us with magical ingredients for everything.

If we're going to explore the magic of the natural world, it's important to also understand the ways in which seasonal rhythms, natural elements, and agricultural cycles influence what we do. Our ancestors, long ago, may not have been Wiccan, but they certainly understood the cycles of the seasons, the changes in the movement of the stars, and the ebb and flow of the tides.

The best way to gain an understanding of practical natural magic is by getting to know the world around you. Spend as much time outdoors as possible, in all kinds of weather. Pick up an almanac and keep track of the phases of the moon. Understand agricultural markers in your own area—when are things planted, and when is the harvest? Get to know the rocks, animals, and plant life near you, and make the effort to appreciate them. Live in an environmentally conscious way whenever you can, because taking care of the land, air, and water in your own community will help you understand them better.

As you work through this book, you'll encounter herbs and crystals that may be unfamiliar to you, and that's okay. You'll get far more out of this information if you take the time to learn how everything ties together, rather than focusing on each herb or crystal as a single, unique item. By the time you're done, you'll not only have a solid foundation for understanding magical theory, you'll also be able to put what you've learned into practice.

There Is a Season, There Is an Element

The changing seasons and the four cardinal elements, as well as their associated correspondences, are integral to Wiccan magic. By understanding the connections between the seasonal agricultural ceremonies and the elements, you'll be better equipped to make natural magic happen.

The Seasons

Fall: During the harvest season, Wiccan rituals focus on reaping what you have sown and gathering abundance. This is the season of thankfulness and gratitude. In addition, it's the period in which the nights are growing longer and darker, and for Wiccans, it's the season of the Witches' New Year, the time in which the cycle of life, death, and rebirth begins anew. The crops and fields are dying, and with them the earth, but we know that despite the end of the harvest, life will return again in a few months.

Winter: For most of us, winter is a fallow time. It's the coldest part of the year, the land is frozen, and the skies are dark and gloomy. However, this is also a season of celebration, when we gather together with our loved ones. We mark the return of the light at the winter solstice, when the sun begins to move closer to the earth, and the days gradually begin to get longer.

Spring: During the spring season, life is beginning anew in the fields and gardens. Spring is a time of planting and fertility, and of the rebirth of the land. It's the time of year when we feel revitalized, as life returns once more. It's the season in which we begin to start thinking about what we want to bring into our own lives as we plant seeds—both physical and spiritual—for our goals for the year. We rejoice in the greening of the earth in spring, and recognize that this is a time of year when we can take advantage of the earth's natural cycles to bring about fruitfulness and creation in our lives.

Summer: In the summer months, the theme is power and energy. The sun is at its peak in the sky, and warmth and light are everywhere. Focus your summer celebrations on strength and power, drawing on the energy of the sun. The days are long and warm, we're outdoors more, and we're staying up later. This is a time of productivity and powerful energy. It's also the season in which our gardens are blooming and blossoming, and we can begin harvesting those crops—both physical and spiritual—that we began tending in the spring. Take some time during the summer months to nourish your personal power, reconnect with the land, and embrace that which you have planted.

The Four Elements

Earth: The element of Earth doesn't just mean the planet itself; it also applies to all the planet's attributes, such as stones, trees, and mountains. Associated with the north, Earth is feminine, fertile, and stable, like the Goddess herself, and tied to the endless cycle of birth, life, death, and finally rebirth. Earth is usually represented by the colors green and brown.

Air: The element of the east, Air is representative of the soul and the breath of life, as well as wisdom and the powers of the mind. Air is the element of communication and can be used to get rid of troublesome issues, carrying them away on the breeze. Air is connected to white and yellow in color magic.

Fire: The masculine, purifying energy of Fire is associated with the God and with the south. It's tied to strong will, passion, and energy. Fire both creates and destroys, and can heal or harm. For color magic, use red and orange for Fire associations.

Water: Used for cleansing and purification, Water is related to the west, and to the Goddess. Water is often associated with blessings, healing, and our emotions. In many Wiccan covens, consecrated water is used to bless the sacred circle and any tools within it. Water is associated with blue in color magic.

Spirit (the optional fifth element): Some Wiccans incorporate a fifth element into their practice, that of Spirit. Although you certainly don't have to, if you choose to work with Spirit, it is generally seen as the Aether, a universal inner space. Spirit is associated with the color white in some Wiccan traditions, although others believe that Spirit has no color at all; it simply *is*. This element is unlike the other four in that it is not connected to a specific direction but to the higher self, the Divine, and the wisdom that can be attained only as we grow and develop spiritually.

"The first time I called myself a 'Witch' was the most magical moment of my life."

—Margot Adler, *Drawing Down the Moon: Witches, Druids, Goddess-Worshippers, and Other Pagans in America*

Revel in Celebration

Wiccan sacred days are known as Sabbats, or days of power. These are tied to the changing seasons and astronomical markers such as the solstices and equinoxes. In addition to the eight Sabbats, there are also monthly Esbats, celebrations of the full moon typically honoring the Goddess. Much like the Sabbats, the Esbats have unique themes based upon the time of the year. *Note: The dates shown are for the Northern Hemisphere; in the Southern Hemisphere, the dates are six months opposite.*

The Sabbats

Samhain (October 31): Known as the Witches' New Year, Samhain is when many Wiccans celebrate the cycle of life, death, and rebirth. It's the season of transformation, associated with the colors black, orange, and purple, all of which are tied to the underworld and the land of the dead. Associated herbs and crystals include rosemary for remembrance; mugwort for divination; cleansing sage, along with amber and hematite, tied to protection; and the banishing power of obsidian.

Yule (December 20–22): The winter solstice marks the beginning of the sun's journey back to earth. Use holly and mistletoe for herbal magic, particularly if you're doing protection workings, and frankincense resin for purification. Include rubies to represent generosity and contentment, garnet for intuition and inner peace, and green tourmaline for prosperity in your crystal workings. Color correspondences for Yule include red, gold, and green, all of which are associated with prosperity and success.

Imbolc (February 2): Imbolc, also called Candlemas, is a time when many Wiccans celebrate the coming end of winter. Herbal magic includes bay laurel and iris, associated with the onset of spring, and violets, a flower of both love and protection. For color magic, use red, connected to passion and fire, and white, representing the snow that blankets the ground. If you're doing crystal workings, include dark gemstones like bloodstone, tied to prosperity, and amethyst and moonstone, which aid in intuition and psychic development.

Ostara (March 20–22): The spring equinox, or Ostara, is a time of balance, of equal hours of light and dark. Welcome the season with soft pastel colors, and include herbs like daffodil, lilac, and willow, all of which begin to bloom in the spring and are associated with new beginnings. Crystal magic for this Sabbat can include agate for healing magic, lapis lazuli for courage and strength, and rose quartz, which comes in handy for love magic.

Beltane (May 1): This fertility festival celebrates the greening of the earth. It's when Wiccan magic focuses on fire and passion, so bold colors like forest green, associated with the earth itself, and bright lusty red come into play. Use herbs like lavender for dream magic, thistle for healing and protection, and dogwood for wishes and good health. This Sabbat's crystal magic includes emerald for fertility and romance, tourmaline for creativity and attraction, and the success and abundance properties of malachite.

Litha (June 20–22): The summer solstice is a time of solar power and energy, so do workings involving midsummer herbs such as basil for calming magic; chamomile, associated with love and marriage; thyme for loyalty; and lemon balm for healing powers. Crystals and gemstones include diamond for love and fidelity, yellow topaz for prosperity, and amber and tiger's eye, both tied to confidence and strength. Color magic focuses on the sun and its bright hues; yellow, red, and bright orange are always appropriate for magical workings at midsummer.

Lammas (August 1): Lammas marks the first grain harvest and is associated with crop colors like gold and light brown. Utilize late summer grains such as wheat and corn, which are associated with protection and luck, along with herbs like sunflower for love and fidelity; grapevine, associated with abundance; and mint for healing and cleansing. For crystal workings, use moss agate, citrine, and obsidian.

Mabon (September 20–22): Like Ostara, the autumnal equinox is a time of balance. This Sabbat places emphasis on gratitude for the bounty of the harvest. Use herbs like sage and cinnamon for wisdom and intuition, and apple blossom, associated with the abundance of the harvest season. For crystal magic, include carnelian for luck and protection, and red jasper for healing. The colors for the fall equinox are associated with the ending of the harvest. Deep brown, rusty red, and rich purple are always appropriate for Mabon, as they are reminiscent of the colors of the late fall crops.

The Esbats

January/Cold Moon: This is the time of year when many of us are stuck indoors because the weather is prohibitive. It's a season of simplification, so try a minimalist approach to your life. Do a thorough cleaning of your physical space, eliminating clutter, and try to do the same thing on a spiritual and emotional level. Work on magic related to physical and spiritual protection, as well as development of the self. Colors include black, white, and silver; these are associated with the long, cold nights when the moon may provide the only illumination. For crystal magic, include hematite for protection and obsidian to help you banish all the things you no longer want or need. Herbal correspondences for the Cold Moon are thistle, birch, and marjoram, which all have protective properties.

February/Quickening Moon: This is the season when our ancestors sat by a dwindling fire in the long dark night and wondered if they and their families would make it until spring. However, they knew this was a time of quickening, as new life and conception took place in anticipation of the coming spring. This month, make plans for the coming year, focus on new beginnings, and anticipate the future. Use purple and blue for color magic related to power and healing. Herbs and crystals include the healing properties of hyssop, amethyst, and jasper; sage and myrrh for protection and purification; and rose quartz for new relationships.

March/Storm Moon: The Storm Moon is aptly named, as March often brings heavy rains and gray skies. As the earth is showered with life-giving water, we know we can look forward to a fertile and healthy growing season. This is a season in which we have equal hours of light and darkness, so it is a time of balance. Celebrate rebirth this month, and welcome spring with the pastel colors associated with new life. Use herbs like dandelion for new beginnings and transformation, and apple blossom for healing and love. When it comes to crystal magic this month, use bloodstone for fertility and abundance, and turquoise for wisdom and intuition.

April/Wind Moon: This is a good time to plant the seeds of change and know that the coming months will allow you to reap what you have sown. It's the season to bring about new endeavors and get rid of old baggage once and for all. Incorporate bright primary colors into your workings, which are associated with decision making, power, and change. Use crystals like quartz and selenite for cleansing and elimination of bad habits. Herbs for April include dandelion and milkweed, associated with transformation, and dill for luck and success.

May/Flower Moon: If you want to be fruitful and abundant, May is the perfect month for fertility magic. Focus on making big changes this month. May's colors include green and red, associated with passion, fire, and the earth itself. Use crystals like emeralds and rubies, tied to prosperity and fruitfulness. For herbal magic, build your workings around herbs such as cinnamon, lavender, and members of the mint family, related to fertility and lust.

June/Strong Sun Moon: In June, work on nurturing your relationships and empowering your spirit with sunny colors—yellow, red, and orange. This is a season of strong personal power, so take advantage of it! Begin considering what bounty you can harvest in your personal life. If you need to reinvent yourself, this is the perfect season for it. Crystal and herbal magic should include topaz and agate for meditation and transformation, along with basil, ferns, and mosses, which are associated with mental clarity, awareness, and decision making.

July/Blessing Moon: This is a time to count your blessings and figure out what you can do to bring even more of them into your life. Work on dream magic and divination in July with the protective properties of herbs like rue and hyssop; lavender and its calming dreams; and chamomile for meditative exercises. Include crystals such as white agate, moonstone, and opals, in addition to silver, white, and pale blue colors, all of which are tied to development of the higher self and personal awareness.

August/Corn Moon: This is the month when the harvest begins to take place, and it's a season to make sacrifices. You may be harvesting this month, but don't forget to make plans for later—what can you set aside for the coming cold season? Heal what might be ailing you before the winter sets in. Color magic this month should include yellow and orange, associated with the late summer grain harvest, along with herbs like rosemary for remembrance, chamomile for its protective properties, and sunflower for a bit of good luck. For crystal workings, use tiger's eye, associated with strength, as well as carnelian and red agate for healing magic.

September/Harvest Moon: The harvest is when we reap what we have sown, so count your blessings! This is the season in which we really begin to stockpile in earnest and celebrate gratitude for hearth and home, and it's also when we notice the nights getting a bit darker. Use earth tones for color magic, in honor of the harvest season and the bounty of the land. Include bloodstone and citrine, associated with abundance, for your crystals this month. Herbal correspondences include wheat for prosperity, witch hazel to ward off negativity, and valerian for protection.

October/Blood Moon: This is the time of year when we really begin to notice how cold and dark the nights are becoming. It's the season in which the veil between our world and that of the spirits grows thin, so it's a good time to work on divination and communication with departed ancestors. Focus on intuition and psychic development this month, using dark colors like burgundy, black, and deep blue, associated with the underworld and the night. Herbal magic should include apple blossom, sweet wormwood, and squash leaves, all of which represent the end of the harvest season. October crystals include darker stones like obsidian for banishing magic, hematite for protection, and bloodstone for guidance.

November/Mourning Moon: It's dark and chilly in November as the days grow even shorter. Use this month to shed yourself of bad habits and the people who make you miserable, and work on developing your relationship with the Divine. Incorporate crystals like lapis lazuli and topaz for calming, meditation, and inner strength as you heal from emotional challenges. For herbal magic, use thistle and betony for protection from evil. For color magic, use grays and blues, reminiscent of the colors of November's skies.

December/Long Nights Moon: As the year winds down and the nights are long, take some time to open your heart and home to others. It's a season for spiritual alchemy; set aside time to seriously evaluate your life, and know that you'll survive the next couple of months of darkness. If you have the resources and will to do so, take your good fortune and share it with others. December's colors are red, associated with fire and passion; white for purity and cleansing; and black, as a reminder of the dark nights. Crystals for this month include turquoise and topaz for meditation and divination. For herbal magic, think seasonally: Mistletoe, holly, and ivy are connected to protection magic and are perfect to use this month to give your family and home an extra layer of magical defense.

Wiccan Rites and Rituals

In addition to the Sabbats and Esbats, Wiccan rituals are often held in honor of various life milestones. At some point, when you feel you're ready to start writing your own rituals, keep these correspondences in mind as a guide. If you don't want to write your own, don't worry! There are expanded directions and sample rituals for many of these celebrations in part 3.

Dedication

If you wish to dedicate yourself to Wicca and the gods, it is something that is often done after a year and a day of studying and practice. A dedication ritual can be performed with opal or moonstone, along with Blessing Oil (see page 138), salt, and rowan or ivy leaves.

Initiation

Similar to a dedication, an initiation is typically performed in a group setting, and is a way of welcoming a new member not only to the Wiccan religion but also to the coven itself. Use the same crystals and herbs for initiation as you would for your dedication ceremony.

Handfasting

A handfasting is a Wiccan marriage ceremony. For this ritual, use crystals representative of love; rose quartz, diamond, and amber are all appropriate. Pink, white, yellow, and gold are a few of the colors associated with marriage. Lavender, basil, and patchouli are the perfect herbs for a handfasting. Sandalwood, rose, or ylang-ylang oils can be used as well to craft a romantic ritual.

Parting of the Ways

When a couple separates or divorces, it's not uncommon to perform a ceremony to mark the occasion. Use camphor or cayenne, associated with unbinding. When it comes to crystals, select aquamarine or labradorite for emotional healing.

Wiccaning

Much like a christening or baptism, a Wiccaning ritual welcomes a new baby into the family and community. Select either earth tones or soft pastel colors. Be sure to avoid using any oils directly on the baby's skin. Crystals associated with new births are amethyst, rose quartz, and moonstone; do not give these to a baby, though, as they can present a choking hazard.

Funerary Rites

The Wiccan view of death includes belief in the afterlife, sometimes called the Summerland. Use mandrake root, pennyroyal, or frankincense in funeral rituals, along with jasmine, geranium, or lavender oils. Crystals associated with death include onyx, amethyst, and Apache tears. Color correspondences include black, dark purple, and dark blue.

The Great Rite: In some Wiccan traditions, a High Priest and High Priestess may participate in the Great Rite, the ritualized sexual union of the God and Goddess. It is typically performed in private by an established adult couple.

Your Daily Wiccan Practice

Following a Wiccan path involves more than simply observing eight Sabbats or celebrating the full moon each month. By getting into the habit of living magically every day, you'll soon be able to incorporate your spirituality into your mundane activities—work, family, school, and everything else. Here are some ways you can live a magical life.

Get in Touch with Nature

We've already talked about the natural world being an extension of the sacred, so if you've never really spent any time getting out in nature, now is a good time to start. Go for a walk in the woods sometime when you can do so undisturbed. Turn off your cell phone, forget about work for a while, leave any distractions at home, and enjoy the sights and sounds of nature. Listen to the birds in the sky above, sniff some flowers, wrap your arms around a tree, and pick up a rock.

Plant a garden. If you don't have a yard, that's all right—try container gardening. Select some magical herbs or flowers that you'd like to grow, dig your hands deep into the soil, and engage in the magical act of planting. Cultivating a seed and bringing forth new life is a great way to get to know our natural world.

Study the stars, the planets, the moon, and the sun. While astrology and planetary correspondences are not specifically Wiccan, understanding these things will give you an even richer foundation upon which to build your later studies. Go outside under a full moon, stand with your arms outstretched, close your eyes, and feel the magic of the moonlight wash over you.

Show Respect to Your Gods

If you're going to work with the gods and goddesses, it's important to take the time to get to know them well. After all, as a Wiccan, you'll probably be spending a lot of time with your deities, so it's worth making the effort to form a respectful relationship with them. If you can't be bothered to do this, you're probably not ready to work with them.

What kind of connection do you want to have with the Divine? Do you want them to simply grant you favors when you need help? Or would you prefer to establish a mutually satisfying relationship in which you work side by side with the god and goddess of your belief system? Get to know the deities by doing some meditation and speaking to them; while they may not answer, they're probably listening.

Set up an altar to your deities in your home, and make sure you keep it tidy and clean. After all, you wouldn't invite your friends into a dirty house, so you certainly shouldn't invite the gods to a messy altar. Your altar should become part of your regular practice. It's more than just a workspace where you keep your magical tools. It's the center of ritual and spellwork, and will become a sacred spot in your home as you learn to celebrate the seasons, make your own magic, and work with your gods. Offer prayers to them each day, whether it's something as simple as lighting a candle and saying hello, or as complex as making an offering while reciting a chant you wrote in their honor.

Consider the Impact of Words and Deeds

Words matter, as do actions. Everything we say and do, whether it's a ritual or spell or a conversation with a family member or coworker, has an impact on other people. In spellwork, in particular, a phrasing that's just a little bit off can throw a monkey wrench into the whole thing. Your life is the same way; speaking without thoughtfulness can cause harm and damage to yourself and to other people. Likewise, your magical actions matter just as much as your non-magical ones, so consider them carefully before you bring them to fruition.

Be Empowered

Have you ever felt completely helpless, as though you had no control at all over the things that were taking place in your life? While you may not always be in control of other people's words and actions, you do have some say in how they make you feel and how you respond to them. This gives you far more agency over your life. If someone or something makes you unhappy, it's okay to focus on self-care. Make the changes that are necessary to find yourself some happiness.

Magic, in its purest form, is about manifesting change in the things we don't like. If we are going to do magic to transform our lives, why wouldn't we also use non-magical behaviors to do the same? You have value, and that gives you strength. Take that strength and use it to empower yourself in every aspect of your day-to-day life.

Embrace Personal Responsibility

Just as you have control over your magical and daily life, you are also responsible for your words and actions. Are you willing to take ownership of everything you do and say? Sometimes this includes admitting you're wrong, which can be a hard thing to do. If you're planning to make magic, you must keep in mind that sometimes the results are not going to be quite what you planned or what you expected. When things go wrong—and any experienced magical practitioner will tell you that eventually something will indeed go wrong—are you willing to acknowledge that you made a mistake? If you can do this in your magical life, you can do it in your mundane life as well.

Live Curiously

It's very important to realize and accept that you don't know everything there is to know. Life is a never-ending journey of discovery, so always be open to learning new things. Ask questions when you don't know something, and understand that sometimes the answers aren't going to be what you wanted to hear. Remember that new knowledge can often come from unexpected sources; don't rule a lesson out just because it came as a surprise to you.

Be willing to think outside the box, and listen to different viewpoints and ideas, even if they don't match up with your own. The more curious you are about the world around you and the people in it, the more able you will be to expand your view of life in general. As your worldview grows, so will your knowledge and, subsequently, your ability to manifest magic in your life.

CHAPTER TWO

The Tools of the Tradition

As you become more familiar with Wiccan practice, you'll see that magical tools can come in handy. From herbs and crystals to the wand and the athame (a ceremonial knife), tools are an important part of magical practice. While you certainly don't *have* to use them—because as you learn and practice more, you'll figure out that you can often make magic without tools—many people find that doing so allows for greater magical focus.

"Nature is only wild to those who separate themselves from her."

—Raven Grimassi, *Grimoire of the Thorn-Blooded Witch: Mastering the Five Arts of Old World Witchery*

Of the Earth

Because Wicca is a nature-based religious system, many of the items used in Wiccan magic are found within nature itself. We'll get into the specifics in the next two chapters, but for now, let's take a brief look at the ways you can incorporate natural items like herbs and crystals, as well as oils and candles, into your workings.

Herbs and Plants

Herbs have been used in magic since the beginning of recorded history. After all, our ancestors didn't have access to today's manufactured resources, so they had to rely upon what their environment provided. Herbs, trees, flowers, and even vegetables became a source for magical ingredients. When you're using herbs and other plants in magic, it's important to do so with a bit of caution; many plants can be handled safely but should not be taken internally. Many people find that the most practical and safe way to use magical herbs is to blend them as incense for ritual, stuff them into a magical doll, create an herbal sachet, or even sprinkle them around the house.

Essential Oils

The use of oils in ritual and ceremony has been documented for thousands of years. For early priests and priestesses, these sacred oils were made by blending fragrant herbs and flowers with melted animal fat. Fortunately, you don't have to melt your own fat to create magical oil blends because you can combine herbs or essential oils with a base, or carrier, oil like grapeseed, jojoba, or even olive oil. Magical oil blends can be used to anoint candles and other items. Be careful when applying oils directly to the skin; some can cause an allergic reaction.

Crystals and Stones

Wicca is just one of many metaphysical belief systems that include the use of crystals. Although few know for certain how they work, many people believe crystals have magical properties, from healing to prosperity to protection. The theory is that each crystal has its own unique vibration or frequency, and these energies can bring about harmony, balance, and change. By carrying or wearing crystals, placing them around your home, or utilizing them in spellwork, you can take advantage of their different magical associations.

Candles

Candle magic is one of the most popular and effective forms of spellwork in Wicca today, and this is due in part to the fact that it's just so simple; anyone can do a basic spell with a candle and little else. Candle spells are a form of sympathetic magic, in which an item—in this case, the candle—stands in as a symbolic representation of something else.

Candle spells work just like any other spell. By setting a goal, visualizing the end result, and then using appropriate candle colors to manifest the desired result, you can bring about change. When you're selecting candles for magical purposes, it's always a good idea to go with a smaller candle than a larger one. Big candles last a long time, and since many spells suggest letting the candle burn out on its own, this can be counterproductive. Instead, select a smaller size like a tea light, a votive, or a four-inch taper for the best results. In addition, be sure to use a brand-new candle for each spell or ritual, unless the working specifically calls for a candle to be relit multiple times.

> **"Most things radiate energy. Often that energy is subtle, but a good Witch nearly always picks up on it. When deciding whether to purchase or use a ritual tool, it's important to 'sense' that energy."**
>
> —Jason Mankey, *The Witch's Athame: The Craft, Lore & Magick of Ritual Blades*

Other Magical Objects and Actions

Herbs, oils, crystals, and candles aren't the only magical items you may find yourself drawn to. In most Wiccan traditions, certain ritual tools are considered an integral part of magic. While many Wiccans will tell you that an experienced practitioner doesn't need any tools at all, you'll probably find that as you learn more about magic theory, it's helpful to use the appropriate tools. In general, it's a good idea to ritually consecrate your magical tools before their first use (see page 170).

Athame: The athame is a ceremonial knife that represents the sacred masculine and is used to direct energy in rituals. Typically a double-edged dagger, the athame can be purchased at just about any metaphysical store. You can make your own, but unless you have skills with an anvil and forge, it's probably easier to buy one. If you don't have an athame, use a wand, your finger, or another knife that is set aside for magical use only.

Book of Shadows: Nearly every Wiccan keeps a Book of Shadows, or BOS, a book that holds spells, rituals, prayers, correspondence tables, and other information useful to magical practice. You can make your Book of Shadows in any blank journal or notebook, but the contents should be personal and unique to you. This is discussed in more detail in appendix C.

Broom: The broom, or besom, is associated with the element of Water and is used for metaphysical cleansing. Use your broom to eliminate negative energies. You can easily make one, but if you choose to purchase a broom, make sure you use it only for magical purposes.

Cauldron: The cauldron is a symbol of the Goddess and the element of Water. Use your cauldron to burn incense or make offerings, or fill it with water and use it for some moonlight scrying, which is a method of divination that involves staring into a reflective surface to see images.

If you burn magical items in your cauldron, it will be unsafe for food; keep a separate cauldron for kitchen use.

Chalice: The cup, or chalice, is often used to represent the womb of the Goddess during a symbolic reenactment of the Great Rite, in which it is paired with the athame. Not everyone owns a chalice, so a bowl is a perfectly acceptable substitution.

Pentacle: The pentacle is a flat piece of wood, metal, clay, or wax inscribed or painted with magical symbols and used on an altar to represent the element of Earth. The most commonly seen symbol is the pentagram, a five-pointed star. Make your own pentacle with a piece of clay or a wooden disc, and some carving tools, paint, or even a wood burning kit.

Robe: Many Wiccans wear robes in ritual because they allow you to walk from the world of the mundane into the world of the magical. You can buy a robe, or you can make one with a few basic sewing skills. If you can't sew and don't want to buy a robe, you don't have to use one, but whatever you do wear in ritual should be designated strictly for magical use.

Wand: Symbolic of the God, the wand is used for directing magical energy. To make your own, go out in the woods. Touch the trees, and feel their spirit. When you find one that resonates with you, look beneath it to see if it has dropped any branches recently. Use one of these as your wand.

In addition to the above, you may want to incorporate music, dancing, and chants into your rituals and celebrations. Try a variety of different songs, movements, or chants to see which resonate with you the most. You can find popular Wiccan songs like "We All Come from the Goddess," "Earth My Body," and "Maiden, Mother, Crone" in abundance online, but it's even better if you can write your own songs to strengthen your personal connection to the Divine.

Where to Find Your Herbs

Herbs and oils are commonly used in Wiccan practice because they're a way of bringing natural elements into your magical workings. You can use them for everything from stuffing magical dolls and sachets to blending incense. You can find many herbs commercially, forage for them in the wild, or grow your own from seeds.

Shopping for Herbs

There are a number of options available to you when you start buying herbs for magical purposes. Whether you choose to purchase them online or from a local shop, there are a few key points to keep in mind. A lot of herbs, especially the ones that might be used in cooking, can be found just about anywhere. Others, which may be rare and harder to track down, may require a bit of research and effort, but your local metaphysical shop should be able to source them for you.

When you buy herbs commercially, regardless of where they come from, make sure that they're stored in a container or bag with an airtight seal. Buy only what you need or what you'll be able to use up in a short period. Herbs degrade over time, which can reduce their magical potency. If you buy too much, you'll just end up having to throw some of it away later.

Harvesting, Drying, and Storing Magical Herbs

Harvesting your own herbs, whether you've grown them yourself or foraged them, can be a gratifying experience. It's up to you whether to collect a few bits at a time, as you need them, and use them fresh, or just gather entire bunches at once to dry and store for later. Some Wiccans use a boline, a type of ritual blade, to harvest herbs, but you can use any tool with a sharp edge; whatever you use, try to make sure your tool is used only for herb harvesting. Cut herbs early in the day, before the sun has dried them out. This allows the herbs to maintain their essential oils, which is an important part of herb use and keeps them fragrant.

To dry your herbs, tie a bundle of them together with string, and hang them in a cool, dry place for three to four weeks, or spread them on a tray in your oven at a low temperature until they are crisp but not burned. To store them, place them in colored glass jars or ceramic containers with airtight lids. Be sure to label each one with the herb's name on it and the date of the harvest. Keep your jars in a cool, dark area.

Charging Your Herbs

In many Wiccan traditions, charging your herbs is a way of filling them with magical energies prior to use in spellwork or ritual. In fact, by blending your own magical energy with that of the herb, you'll get them ready for magical use. Some of the most popular methods involve placing them outside under the moonlight or sunlight. Some people prefer to use moonlight to charge items for magic related to inner growth, such as intuition, wisdom, and healing, and use sunlight for magic associated with strength and power, but there isn't any hard-and-fast rule on this.

In general, herbs shouldn't be left out for extended periods in direct sunlight, but you can charge them by placing them outside for short periods on sunny days. Another simple and efficient method of charging your herbs is by holding them in your hands while meditating, or chanting as you focus your magical intent upon them.

Kitchen Herbs for Magical Use

You can absolutely incorporate cooking herbs into magical use! Kitchen herbs and spices like basil, cinnamon, rosemary, and sage all have magical applications as well as culinary ones. Don't rule out an herb's efficacy in spellwork just because you found it at the grocery store. Also, keep in mind that kitchen magic, which we'll discuss in more detail later in this chapter, is a great way to bring spellwork into your day-to-day life.

Essential Oil Blends

Many Wiccans purchase essential oils for magic, but it's important to keep in mind that some of them should be used with caution. Don't ingest an essential oil or apply it directly on your skin without doing your homework first. You can create your own blends for a variety of magical purposes by adding a few drops of one or two essential oils into a few

Growing and Wildcrafting Your Magical Herbs

For most of us, it's simply more practical to purchase the magical items we need. However, if you have the ability and desire to grow your own herbs or go foraging for them, it's more than a good way to save money. It's also a great opportunity to get more involved in the magical process from start to finish. After all, what's more magical than bringing forward new life on your own?

To grow your own herbs, start with seeds in small containers. Most beginners find that the best way to get familiar with herb gardening is to select a few that are easy to grow with a minimal amount of work. Rosemary, sage, basil, and members of the mint family are all incredibly simple to grow and maintain. Try a few of these, and once they're flourishing in pots indoors, transfer them to your garden to grow.

Wildcrafting is the practice of collecting herbs and plants from their natural habitat. Doing so ethically and responsibly allows plants to continue to grow in a way that's sustainable. Get permission from property owners before you go wildcrafting on their land, and always make sure you carry a guide to your region's plant resources. Try to collect herbs from areas that will not be noticeably damaged if you do so, only take what you need, and offer thanks to the gods of your tradition before you walk away with your harvest.

ounces of a base oil like unscented grapeseed or jojoba oil. From there, you can create your own magical oils for blessing, prosperity, protection, and more.

Kitchen Magic

If you're following a Wiccan path, you'll soon come to recognize why, for many of us, the kitchen is the heart of spellwork and magic. Kitchen witchcraft is a way to incorporate the magical into mundane tasks like meal preparation; by ritualizing your cooking process, you can infuse your will and intent into every dish you serve.

Have a Kitchen Altar

We'll talk shortly about setting up a magical altar in your home, but the kitchen is a great place to start doing this. Welcome the gods and goddesses into your home with small statues and symbols in your kitchen, add a cauldron or an unscented candle, or even paint trivets and coasters with magical images to place in your kitchen. Your kitchen should be a place of joy and comfort, so personalize it in a way that makes you feel magical! Small, portable items make for a great kitchen altar; place them on a tray so you can move them out of the way if you're short on space.

Create Sacred Space

If your kitchen is a place where you're going to make magic happen, it should be treated accordingly. Keep the room physically tidy and free of clutter and dirt; the best way to do this is by cleaning as you go instead of letting things pile up. Paint the walls and cabinets in colors that make you and your family feel relaxed and happy. Read up on feng shui practices so you can organize your kitchen for maximum efficiency.

Cook with Magical Intent

When you cook, do you pay attention to the direction in which you stir? Move your spoon in a *deosil*, or sunwise, direction to attract magic toward you. Stir the opposite way, or *widdershins*, to banish or eliminate things from your life. When you're frosting a cake, decorating a cookie, or even adding condiments to a sandwich, use ingredients to create magical symbols like dollar signs for money, hearts for love, or a shield for protection. Add herbs and spices that correspond to your magical intentions when you're making a dish to eat, and focus on that intent as your meal is cooking.

Keep Things Convenient

The more accessible the magical tools in your kitchen are, the more likely you are to use them. Make sure herbs and spices are organized and easy to find; you can even display them in decorative, labeled jars. If you have a special spoon—and wooden spoons come in very handy in the kitchen—that you like to use, make sure it's always within reach. For some witches, the spoon is practically a substitute for the wand. Keep cookbooks at your fingertips, and keep live herbs on the counter to use all year long in your magical cooking.

Magical Crystals and Gemstones

There are hundreds of magical crystals and gemstones to choose from, but the ones you will want to use depend on your goals. Choose crystals to work with based upon their correspondences, or attributes, and you can't go wrong. In the next section, we'll look at some of the most popular crystals and gemstones used in magical workings and rituals, as well as ideas for how you can incorporate them into practice. Before we do, though, let's go over a few things to keep in mind.

Where to Find Your Crystals

Sourcing magical crystals isn't quite as easy as finding herbs, simply because you can't exactly grow your own or just wander off to the woods to find what you need. However, in many states, you can find places that allow you to mine and hunt for your own crystals, so look into this if you've got the time and the money. If you don't have access to this resource, take the time to get to know the staff at your local metaphysical shop, and ask them how and where they buy their crystals for resale.

Ask questions to make sure their crystals are not acquired from companies that use child labor or harmful environmental practices. Another great option is to attend a gem convention near you so that you can interact with people who truly love crystals and stones, and who can tell you more about an item's origins.

Cleansing and Charging

As with most other magical tools, it's a good idea to do a thorough metaphysical cleansing on your crystals before you use them the first time. There are different methods you can use, and these will vary depending on the type of crystal you're working with. You may wish to perform a full-fledged consecration ritual like the one described in chapter 7, or you can keep things simple. Leave your crystals out in the moonlight for three nights, or use sage or other purification herbs to smudge them. You can even use consecrated water to cleanse your crystals, but don't ever immerse them in hot water; this can cause some types of crystals to crack.

Crystal Therapy

Many people believe that crystals have more than just metaphysical properties; they are often used in healing modalities as well. By carrying crystals on your person, wearing them as jewelry, or even placing them around your home, you can tap into their therapeutic vibrations to bring about wellness and health.

Negative Reactions to Crystals

Some people actually report feeling a negative reaction to certain crystals. Although this is an uncommon phenomenon, it does happen. If you find that working with a specific crystal makes you feel anxious or lightheaded, stop using it, and substitute something with similar properties.

Candles and Colors

Candle magic is one of the most popular forms of Wiccan spellwork and ritual, because not only is it easy, it's effective. This very basic method of sympathetic magic doesn't require fancy tools or elaborate lists of supplies; a few tea lights or votive candles in a variety of colors can be all you need to get started.

Most Wiccan traditions hold to a general standard of color correspondences, but it's also acceptable to use personal variations as needed. Use red for passion, lust, and sexual love, but pink for sweet and platonic love or friendship. Gold and green both come in handy for financial endeavors and abundance, while various shades of blue are associated with health, patience, and understanding. For workings related to ambition and power, use purple candles. Use orange and yellow for attraction, persuasion, and protection. The color brown is associated with the earth and can be used in workings related to animals or the land. Black is the color of banishment and negativity, while silver is connected to lunar energy, wisdom, and intuition. Finally, white is useful as a color of purity and truth, but in many magic traditions, it is acceptable to substitute white for any other color.

Your Magical Altar

The altar is the place where Wiccans make magic happen; it is the focus of religious ceremony, and it's a workspace where you can perform spell-work with all your magical tools at hand. In many Wiccan traditions, there is significance to the positioning and placement of magical tools on the altar.

Symbols of the Elements

Items to represent the four elements are placed on the altar in alignment with the four directions on the compass. Earth can be represented by a bowl of sand, salt, or soil, and placed on the north side of the altar. Use a feather or a stick of incense on the east side to symbolize Air, and a candle or charcoal representing Fire on the south side. Finally, on the west side of the altar, place a cup or bowl of water, or even a seashell. If you don't have access to any of these things, don't worry. You can also use candles to represent the elements—brown or green for Earth, yellow or pink for Air, orange or red for Fire, and blue for Water. If you're working with the fifth element, Spirit, you can place that item in the center of the altar.

The God and Goddess

Add symbols of the God and Goddess of your tradition to the altar. Place these as centrally as possible or even on an elevated level above the rest of the altar tools—after all, they're deities and should be placed in a position of honor. You can use statues or items that symbolize the deities if you have them. For instance, a set of horns can be used to represent the God, and a lunar symbol can be used in honor of the Goddess. As with the elements, you can also use candles to represent the deities, marking them with specific deity symbols.

Magical Tools

Your altar should have plenty of room for your magical tools, but there's no need to clutter it up with the ones you're not using. The athame and wand are typically placed to the right of the altar for easy access, and the Book of Shadows to the left, but if you're left-handed, it's perfectly okay to switch these. In addition to your basic magical tools, you'll want to include items that are specific to the ritual you're performing or the Sabbat you're celebrating. Decorate your altar with seasonal flowers, plants, stones and crystals, cakes and ale, and so forth. Whatever you're placing on the altar, make sure you've got everything you need easily available before you begin your ritual.

Invoking the Quarters

In some Wiccan groups, the quarters are called. This is a process in which the High Priestess or Priest invokes guardians, or watchtowers, to preside over the space. If you want to use this method, you can move around the circle, beginning at the north, and work in a clockwise direction. As you reach each point in the circle, stop and raise your hands to the sky, holding your athame or wand, and speak these words: *Watch-towers of the [Direction], Guardians of [Element], I call upon you to join this sacred circle. Keep that which is good within, and prevent anything negative from entering this space. So mote it be.*

Calling Upon the Deities

In other traditions, the God and Goddess themselves are called upon to join in the sacred circle. This is a way of inviting them to be part of the ritual, and if you're new to working with deities, it's a good way to get to know them better. To do this, walk the circle's perimeter—again, beginning at the north and moving clockwise—and stop at each point. As you pause at the north, east, south, and west, say, *I call upon the God and Goddess, with the powers of the [Direction], to join me in this sacred ritual. You are honored here, and you are welcomed. So mote it be.*

Casting a Sacred Circle: In traditional Wicca, a circle is cast to create sacred space. This has a twofold purpose: It keeps good energy contained within, and negative energy kept outside. It's a good idea to get in the habit of casting a circle before ritual so that you get familiar with the process. Use the ritual on page 157 to easily cast a circle for ritual and spellwork.

PART II

Guide to Herbs, Oils, and Crystals

"Here's a tip to personalize your spiritual or magical activities: Choose a signature herb or stone and add it to all your magical work. Enchant it with your personal energy first: Hold and visualize your personal energy flowing from your heart down your arms to your hands, and being absorbed by the herbs or stone."

—Arin Murphy-Hiscock, *The Way of the Hedge Witch: Rituals and Spells for Hearth and Home*

While there are thousands of herbs, oils, and crystals you could use in magical practice, we'll look at the most commonly used ones to get you started. Each item discussed will include a list of magical associations and ritual applications, as well as appropriate substitutions where relevant. Whether you're doing a working for healing, love, prosperity, or to develop your own intuition, the possibilities are endless, and you're limited only by your own imagination.

CHAPTER THREE
Herbs and Oils

U sing herbs and oils in magical practice is an essential way to reconnect with nature and the Divine. By incorporating elements of the natural world into our magical practice, we bring ourselves closer to the gods and can create much more effective magic. In this chapter, we'll explore 30 of the most commonly used herbs and oils found in magical practice today.

Cost Key

$ $5 or less per ounce

$$ $5 to $10 per ounce

$$$ $10 or more per ounce

In mythology, apples are associated with immortality and health, and an apple branch bearing unopened blossoms was considered a magical key to the land of the dead. Apple blossoms are also associated with love magic, as well as themes of fertility, prosperity, and abundance. You can certainly buy these commercially, but if you have access to an apple tree, gathering the blossoms in the spring is a great way to add to your herbal magic collection.

Cost: $

Parts Used: Flowers, leaves

Associated Element: Water

Magical Uses: Abundance, fertility, health, immortality, love, prosperity

Rituals and Celebrations: Love magic, spring celebrations

Blends Well With: Comfrey for healing, cinnamon and patchouli for love

Substitutions: Rosebuds, vanilla, young violets

Often Used With: Bloodstone, carnelian, Shiva Lingam

Applications: Add blossoms to incense for love magic, or carry in a sachet for fertility and abundance. Steep them in warm water to create a skin wash for youthful beauty. Hang garlands over your bed for fertility. Dress a green candle with oil and crushed apple blossoms for a simple money spell, or place the flowers in your wallet or purse for prosperity.

Precautions: No known precautions.

You're probably familiar with basil as a cooking herb, but it also comes in handy for a number of magical applications. Associated with purification and good fortune in the home, basil can also appear in love magic, particularly in matters of fidelity and loyalty. Bake basil into a loaf of bread or a pasta dish and feed it to someone whom you'd like to remain loyal. Basil oil can be blended with other calming oils in a base to help alleviate emotional stress or mental fatigue.

Cost: $

Parts Used: Essential oil, leaves

Associated Element: Fire

Magical Uses: Calming, fidelity, good luck, love, purification

Rituals and Celebrations: Love divination, purification rituals

Blends Well With: Lemon and rosemary to relieve anxiety, peppermint oil to spray into the shoes for an energy boost

Substitutions: Coriander, ginger

Often Used With: Bloodstone, diamond, emerald

Applications: Sprinkle dried basil around a lover's side of the bed to keep them from straying. Add a pot of fresh basil to a new home to bring good fortune inside. Scatter the leaves across windows and doorways for purification. Dilute the essential oil in a base oil and dab a bit behind your ears to ignite the fires of passion in your lover!

Precautions: Basil oil can be a stimulant and shouldn't be used by pregnant women or children.

Catnip is a fairly mild herb, and if you give it to your feline companion, some people believe it can help strengthen the psychic bond between you. Popular for use in animal magic, catnip is also associated with love magic. Additionally, catnip's calming properties can be used to alleviate anxious moods—after all, just watch how mellow your cat is after ingesting it!

Cost: $$
Parts Used: Leaves
Associated Element: Water
Magical Uses: Animal magic, calming energy, good luck, love, purification
Rituals and Celebrations: Consecration rituals
Blends Well With: Rose petals for love magic
Substitutions: Comfrey, mint, pennyroyal
Often Used With: Emerald, topaz
Applications: Grow catnip near your home to attract good spirits (and neighborhood cats). Place the leaves in a sachet for love magic, or brew them in water to create a face wash for use in beauty spells. Rub the dried leaves between your hands to help reduce anxiety, or roll a brown candle in catnip for workings related to calming an agitated pet.
Precautions: Large quantities of catnip can promote menstruation, so it should not be ingested by pregnant women.

CHAMOMILE Matricaria chamomilla

The two most common types of chamomile are the Roman and German varieties. Used for centuries for purification and protection, this all-purpose plant is also useful in incense blends for meditation and in teas for restful sleep. In a number of folk magic traditions, chamomile is associated with good luck. It can also be used to prevent magical or psychic attack. Also, although it is associated with the element of Water, chamomile and its bright yellow-and-white flowers are also strongly connected to the energy of the sun.

Cost: $$
Parts Used: Essential oil, flowers, leaves
Associated Element: Water
Magical Uses: Good luck, meditation, protection from evil, purification
Rituals and Celebrations: Litha celebrations, sun magic
Blends Well With: Comfrey or peppermint for healing or cleansing, sandalwood for meditation
Substitutions: Heliotrope, sunflower
Often Used With: Amber, amethyst, hematite, jet, obsidian, onyx
Applications: Blend chamomile into a tea before bed for calm sleep, or burn it as incense for meditative rituals. Want to protect your family from negative magic? Plant the flowers around your home. You can also carry the dried blossoms in your pocket as a good-luck charm.
Precautions: Do not use chamomile if you are pregnant, allergic to ragweed and/or pollen, or taking any blood-thinning or anticoagulant medications.

Today, we use cinnamon primarily as a culinary ingredient. However, our ancient ancestors used it in a number of different religious capacities. Cinnamon oil was used in Egypt as part of funerary rites, and Roman priests decorated many of their temples with the leaves. Cinnamon is associated with fiery passion, so use it in magic related to love and lust, as well as for psychic abilities, personal power, and success.

Cost: $$

Parts Used: Bark, essential oil

Associated Element: Fire

Magical Uses: Ambition, passionate love, power, psychic development, success

Rituals and Celebrations: Fertility rites, Yule celebrations

Blends Well With: Basil for passion, lavender for psychic clarity

Substitutions: Basil, patchouli, or peppermint for love or passion

Often Used With: Bloodstone, emerald, garnet, jasper, tiger's eye

Applications: Add a bit of the essential oil to a base oil and anoint your wrists with it to spice up your love life. Dress a red candle in oil and roll it in cinnamon for lust spells! Carry cinnamon sticks for magic related to business success and power, sprinkle cinnamon around your home for protection, or place a bit of cinnamon and lavender in a sachet and tuck it into your pillow for psychic development while you sleep.

Precautions: Pregnant and nursing women should avoid using cinnamon oil, as should anyone who has been treated for stomach ulcers.

COMFREY *Symphytum officinale*

Comfrey has a number of magical uses and has been used in folk magic for a long time. If you're heading out on a road trip, take a cue from early travelers. They believed that carrying a bit of comfrey would keep them safe on pilgrimages. Tucking a few leaves in a suitcase or bag is thought to prevent potential loss or tampering. Comfrey is also associated with healing, cleansing, and smudging, as well as divination and prophecy. Add comfrey to a ritual fire for use with divination and scrying, or tuck it under your pillow for restful sleep and relaxing dreams.

Cost: $

Parts Used: Leaves

Associated Element: Water

Magical Uses: Cleansing, divination, healing, prophecy, protection, purification

Rituals and Celebrations: Samhain celebrations, scrying and other divination rituals

Blends Well With: Chamomile, feverfew, or yarrow for healing

Substitutions: Mugwort, rosemary, sage

Often Used With: Diamond, obsidian

Applications: Place comfrey in your luggage when you travel to keep your bags from getting stolen, or sprinkle a bit of the leaves in your shoes to make sure you reach your destination safely. Blend a decoction by steeping fresh leaves in warm water and washing with it for protection, or burn as incense for meditation and divination.

Precautions: Keep away from pets, as comfrey can be toxic to them.

DANDELION *Taraxacum officinale*

Dandelions are weeds, but they come in handy for magic. Harvest the flowers, leaves, and even the seed puffs for magical workings. Use dandelions in workings related to divination, psychic development, and personal transformation. Dandelions are also associated with hardiness and resilience, so if you need to do a bit of magic related to strength and stability, dandelion is an excellent spell component.

Cost: $

Parts Used: Flowers, leaves, roots, seed puffs, stems

Associated Element: Air

Magical Uses: Divination, prophetic dreams, strength and stability, transformation

Rituals and Celebrations: Beltane celebrations, rituals involving transformation and new beginnings

Blends Well With: Comfrey or mugwort for divination, holly or thistle for strength

Substitutions: Buttercup, clover, violet

Often Used With: Carnelian, Shiva Lingam

Applications: Brew dandelion leaves into a tea to drink at bedtime for prophetic dreams, or use the seed puffs to blow away your problems. Dry out the flowers and use them in an herbal sachet to keep your home life stable. You can also decorate your altar with the flowers to give your spring spellwork an added boost.

Precautions: No known precautions.

Found in most of Europe and North America, feverfew is a small flowering plant that is similar in appearance to the daisy. The Egyptians and Greeks used it in medicine and found it useful in treating everything from menstrual cramps to the plague to general inflammation. It's a highly effective ingredient in healing magic, as well as in spells for preventing ailments and accidents.

Cost: $$
Parts Used: Flowers, leaves
Associated Element: Water
Magical Uses: Healing, protection from accidents and illness
Rituals and Celebrations: Healing rituals
Blends Well With: Comfrey for healing magic, hyssop and rosemary to prevent accidents
Often Used With: Agate, hematite, jasper, tiger's eye
Applications: Carry feverfew in a sachet if you're going to be around someone who's ill, or blend it into your bathwater and have a good long soak to prevent accidents when you go out. Hang a bundle of feverfew from your rearview mirror to stay safe while driving your car.
Precautions: Anyone who is pregnant, taking any blood-thinning or anti-coagulant medication, or planning surgery should not ingest feverfew.

Goldenseal is known as an herb of attraction, so it comes in very handy indeed when you need to do a bit of money magic. It's also useful in healing rituals and can be burned as incense during meditation. Goldenseal has the additional bonus of being something that gives other workings a boost; add it into any spell for a bit of extra magical energy.

Cost: $$
Parts Used: Flowers, leaves, roots
Associated Element: Fire
Magical Uses: Money, healing
Rituals and Celebrations: Healing rituals, fall celebrations
Blends Well With: Mandrake or pennyroyal for prosperity, rosemary or rue for the element of Fire
Substitutions: Barberry, grape root
Often Used With: Emerald, lodestone
Applications: Create an infusion of goldenseal root in warm water, and sprinkle it around your business for financial success, or keep the leaves and flowers in your wallet or purse to draw money. Burn some as an incense in a sickroom to get rid of illness, or anoint a blue candle with oil and goldenseal powder for general health and well-being.
Precautions: Goldenseal should not be used internally by pregnant or nursing women, or by children.

HOLLY *Ilex aquifolium*

Holly is an evergreen plant that serves all year long as a reminder of the immortality of nature. The Celts considered holly to be a symbol of masculine energy and firmness, and a number of ancient societies used the wood of the holly in the construction of weapons and in protective magic. You may not be using it to build weapons, but you can certainly use it as part of your magical defense system!

Cost: $

Parts Used: Berries, leaves

Associated Element: Fire

Magical Uses: Protection, masculine energy, strength

Rituals and Celebrations: Yule/winter solstice celebrations

Blends Well With: Dandelion or thistle for strength, thistle or tobacco for protection

Substitutions: Mistletoe, rosemary

Often Used With: Hematite, jet, onyx, topaz

Applications: Hang a sprig of holly in your house, or plant a few bushes outside your door to ensure good luck and safety to your family. Dry and powder the leaves and burn as incense, or make holly water by soaking the leaves overnight in spring water under a full moon; then sprinkle the water around the house for blessings, protection, and cleansing.

Precautions: Holly should not be taken internally by pregnant or nursing women, or by anyone who suffers from liver damage. Keep the plants away from children and pets, as both the leaves and berries can be toxic.

The ancient Greeks used hyssop to cleanse and purify their temples; it is associated with the elimination of negativity. It is also used as a healing herb, and during the Renaissance era, Europeans kept hyssop in their sickrooms, both to aid in healing and to mask unpleasant aromas. Use hyssop for workings related to health and wellness, protection, purification, and banishment of negative energy. Hyssop is a fairly easy plant to grow, so keep a pot in your home if possible.

Cost: $$
Parts Used: Essential oil, leaves
Associated Element: Fire
Magical Uses: Banishing, healing, protection, purification
Rituals and Celebrations: Banishing rituals, healing magic
Blends Well With: Feverfew, rue
Substitutions: Rue, pennyroyal, lemon balm
Often Used With: Agate
Applications: Hang hyssop or keep plants in your home to rid the house of negativity, or carry a bit in your pocket for protection. Infuse the leaves in water to sprinkle around the room of someone who is sick, or blend them into incense to purify the home. Anoint a black candle with hyssop essential oil to banish harmful people from your life.
Precautions: Keep hyssop out of reach of pets, as it can be toxic to animals.

LAVENDER *Lavandula angustifolia*

The ancients used lavender in perfumed bathwater and for strewing on the floors of temples and houses. It found its way to England in the 1600s and was even mentioned in the works of William Shakespeare. Lavender essential oil can be incorporated into healing magic and can also be used to bring about peaceful sleep and dreaming. In addition, it is associated with love, cleansing, and purification.

Cost: $$

Parts Used: Essential oil, flowers

Associated Element: Air

Magical Uses: Cleansing, health and wellness, love, purification, sleep and dreams

Rituals and Celebrations: Beltane and other spring celebrations

Blends Well With: Vervain and mint for purification, mugwort for calm dreaming

Substitutions: Fennel, sage

Often Used With: Amethyst, jet

Applications: Blend a few drops of lavender oil into a base oil and apply to your wrists to draw love your way. Make a smudging wand from the flowers and stems, and burn it to purify and cleanse a space. Tuck lavender into your pillow to bring about calm sleep. Steep the flowers in water to create a cooling cleanse for use when you are sick.

Precautions: Exercise caution if you're applying the essential oil to the skin—some people do experience a negative reaction.

LEMON BALM *Melissa officinalis*

As part of the mint family, lemon balm is an easy herb to grow and can be used to make a light and refreshing summer tea. However, it also has a number of magical purposes, including love charms and spells, healing rituals, and development of your psychic abilities. If you choose to grow your own, keep it in a pot—lemon balm will run wild if left to its own devices.

Cost: $$

Parts Used: Leaves

Associated Element: Water

Magical Uses: Love, healing, psychic development

Rituals and Celebrations: Healing rituals, Litha/summer solstice celebrations

Blends Well With: Hyssop or lavender for healing, mugwort for psychic development

Substitutions: Mint, verbena

Often Used With: Clear quartz, garnet, hematite

Applications: For use in healing magic, dress a yellow candle in oil and roll it in dried and powdered lemon balm leaves to tap into the power of the sun for an energy boost, or use it with a blue candle for rituals related to mental health issues. Place the leaves under the pillow of someone who is sick to fend off illness.

Precautions: Lemon balm may occasionally cause drowsiness when ingested by people taking certain medications such as sedatives or insulin; check with your healthcare professional before taking lemon balm internally.

LILAC *Syringa vulgaris*

Lilacs bloom for just a few short weeks in the spring, and their rich, heavy scent is bound to attract your attention. If you have a chance to harvest the flowers yourself, do so, and dry them for magical use later. Lilac is associated with love and romance, particularly new, flirtatious relationships. It is also used in banishing rituals, both to eliminate negative energy and to get rid of pesky, malevolent spirits. Use the dried flowers or fresh flowers for magical workings.

Cost: $$

Parts Used: Branches, flowers

Associated Element: Water

Magical Uses: Banishing negativity, love, new romance, playful flirtation

Rituals and Celebrations: Banishing rituals, Ostara celebrations

Blends Well With: Pennyroyal or rue for banishing, sunflower or valerian for love

Substitutions: Daffodil, forsythia

Often Used With: Emerald, obsidian, onyx, rose quartz

Applications: Harvest a lilac branch to use as a wand in rituals related to love magic, or blend fresh blossoms into a base oil and anoint your wrists to bring romance into your life. Grow a few lilac bushes on your property to keep away anyone who might do you harm, or cut a few fresh blossoms to keep indoors as a way of preventing malevolent spirits from hanging around your home.

Precautions: No known precautions.

MANDRAKE *Mandragora officinarum*

There are multiple types of mandrake plants, but the most commonly found is *Mandragora officinarum*, which has been used in magic and medicine since classical times. Mandrake root became popular in the Middle Ages as a talisman against evil spirits or weapons. Mandrake is sometimes used as an ingredient in lust spells and sex magic, since it is known to have aphrodisiac properties. Carry the root in your pocket, or use the dried leaves in a sachet.

Cost: $$$
Parts Used: Leaves, roots
Associated Element: Fire
Magical Uses: Gambling and money, lust, protection
Rituals and Celebrations: Protection rituals
Blends Well With: Apple blossom or pennyroyal for prosperity, tobacco or valerian for protection
Substitutions: American mandrake (*Podophyllum peltatum*, aka may-apple), bryony
Often Used With: Carnelian, jasper, Shiva Lingam, smoky quartz
Applications: Bury a mandrake root under your doorstep to keep intruders away, or steep the leaves in water and sprinkle this infusion around your property as a protective measure. Because the roots are similar in shape to a human figure, they can be used for any sort of sympathetic magic in which you need a magical doll.
Precautions: Mandrake is highly toxic and should never be ingested; it is a heavy narcotic and can cause miscarriage, hallucinations, or cardiac problems.

MISTLETOE *Viscum album*

Early Greek physicians used mistletoe to treat tumors and epilepsy, but it was the Druids who really got the mistletoe magic going by feeding the leaves to cattle to guarantee fertility. Our modern tradition of kissing under the mistletoe may stem from the Romans, who held fertility rites beneath mistletoe plants. During the Middle Ages, mistletoe once again became popular in both medicine and folk magic. Twigs were hung in bundles to ward off demons, and it was also used to protect livestock from malevolent sorcery.

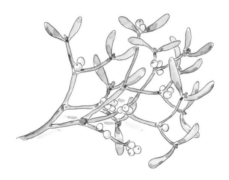

Cost: $$

Parts Used: Flowers, leaves

Associated Element: Air

Magical Uses: Healing, fertility, protection

Rituals and Celebrations: Litha/summer solstice, Yule/winter solstice

Blends Well With: Apple blossom and peppermint for healing, basil and hyssop for protection

Substitutions: Holly

Often Used With: Shiva Lingam

Applications: Place leaves in a pouch to tuck under the bed of a sick person or to be carried by a woman who's having trouble conceiving. Hang a bundle of mistletoe in your home to bring love and abundance your way, or to end strife and discord in your family. Dress a blue candle in dried, powdered mistletoe leaves to burn for healing magic.

Precautions: Mistletoe berries are poisonous and can be fatal if ingested. Pregnant and nursing women should avoid using mistletoe altogether.

MUGWORT *Artemisia vulgaris*

Mugwort has a number of magical uses and is often associated with divination and dreaming; overactive dreams can be balanced out with a ritual bath made from mugwort before bedtime. For prophecy and divination, make an incense of mugwort or use it in smudge sticks around your altar. Mugwort is often associated with the female reproductive system and women's intuition because of its close connections to the moon.

Cost: $

Parts Used: Essential oil, leaves

Associated Element: Earth

Magical Uses: Divination, intuition, psychic development, women's mysteries

Rituals and Celebrations: Litha/summer solstice, solar rituals, lunar celebrations

Blends Well With: Lavender for calm dreaming, lemon balm for psychic development

Substitutions: Comfrey, sage, tobacco

Often Used With: Bloodstone, clear quartz, diamond, garnet, moonstone, turquoise

Applications: Place mugwort under your pillow to prevent psychic attacks in your sleep or to ward off negative dreams, or plant it in your yard to attract fairies. Create a magic broom with mugwort woven into it, and use it to sweep negativity from your home. For a bit of magical defense around your house and property, dab the essential oil on your doors.

Precautions: Pregnant women should not take mugwort internally, as it can lead to miscarriage.

PATCHOULI *Pogostemon cablin*

Patchouli is associated with love, wealth, and sexual power, and can be used in all kinds of magical workings. Wear patchouli oil if you want to attract a lover, but be sure to dilute it with a base oil—a little bit of patchouli goes a long way! If you'd rather not use the oil, place the dried leaves in a sachet, and wear it around your neck or carry it in your pocket.

Cost: $$$
Parts Used: Essential oil, leaves
Associated Element: Earth
Magical Uses: Love, lust, power and wealth, protection
Rituals and Celebrations: Love magic, protection rituals
Blends Well With: Apple blossom or cinnamon for love and passion, golden-seal or pennyroyal for prosperity
Substitutions: Cinnamon, peppermint
Often Used With: Jasper, Shiva Lingam
Applications: Use the leaves in a sachet to draw love your way or if you'd like to give your sex life a boost. Draw a dollar sign in your wallet with the oil for prosperity magic. If you're concerned about harmful energy interfering with your happiness or health, anoint your windows and doors with the oil or scatter the leaves nearby for protection.
Precautions: Do not apply the essential oil directly to the skin because it can cause a reaction. Be sure to dilute it with a base oil first.

In some forms of American folk magic, pennyroyal is associated with money, while in others it is used for protection against hexes. Press fresh flowers and add them to a base oil, and use it to ward off negative magic around your home. Dry out the leaves and use them in an incense blend to protect pets, gardens, and even your car from damage and accidents.

Cost: $
Parts Used: Essential oil, leaves
Associated Element: Fire
Magical Uses: Banishing, money and wealth, protection
Rituals and Celebrations: Banishing rituals
Blends Well With: Goldenseal for prosperity
Substitutions: Comfrey, mint
Often Used With: Jet, obsidian, onyx
Applications: Tuck pennyroyal leaves into your purse or hang them over a cash register at work to bring money into your life, or steep the leaves in water to make a wash for your hands as a way of welcoming prosperity. You can burn pennyroyal leaves as incense around your home to protect your property, or anoint your shoes with the essential oil to keep you safe when traveling.
Precautions: Pennyroyal can be toxic to pregnant women and should not be used in any form by pregnant or nursing women.

PEPPERMINT *Mentha piperita*

The people of ancient Greece and Rome decorated their feasting tables with sprigs of peppermint, and peppermint is also included in Egyptian healing papyri (ancient Egyptian texts). A natural stimulant, peppermint is an easy plant to grow, so start a pot of your own; be careful putting it in the garden, though, as it tends to spread enthusiastically if untended. Use peppermint in rituals for healing and purification, as well as to bring passionate love into your life.

Cost: $

Parts Used: Essential oil, leaves

Associated Element: Fire

Magical Uses: Healing, love, passion, purification

Rituals and Celebrations: Purification and healing rituals

Blends Well With: Sage or sandalwood for cleansing and purification, mistletoe or yarrow for healing

Substitutions: Catnip, comfrey

Often Used With: Agate, tiger's eye

Applications: Rub peppermint leaves on objects to clear them of negative energies, or brew the leaves into a tea to bring about healing and wellness. Add a few drops of the essential oil to a base oil and anoint your wrists and neck to bring passion back into your love life, or if you're hoping to find a new romance, anoint a pink candle with peppermint oil.

Precautions: Peppermint oil can cause a skin reaction in some users and can be toxic if ingested in large quantities, so exercise caution.

Ancient practitioners were familiar with rosemary as an herb of memory. It later became associated with lovers' fidelity and was a popular gift for wedding guests. Rosemary was common in kitchen gardens and represented the dominance of the lady of the house. Roman priests burned rosemary as incense in religious ceremonies, and it is sometimes used for protection from evil spirits even today.

Cost: $$
Parts Used: Essential oil, leaves
Associated Element: Fire
Magical Uses: Fidelity, protection, remembrance
Rituals and Celebrations: Funeral and memorial rituals, marriage ceremonies
Blends Well With: Juniper for healing
Substitutions: Frankincense
Often Used With: Jet, topaz
Applications: Burn rosemary to rid a home of negativity or as incense while you meditate. Hang bundles on your front door to keep danger away. Want to take advantage of this plant's medicinal benefits? Fill a healing doll with dried rosemary. Anoint a white candle with rosemary oil for use in a farewell ritual for the dead.
Precautions: In general, rosemary is not considered toxic; however, the essential oil should be diluted in a base oil before applying to the skin.

Rue is well known as an herb for use in breaking curses, hexes, or any other magical mayhem that may be coming your way. It can be used in exorcisms, to cast out hostile spirits, or to send malevolent magic back to its point of origin. Hang rue in your home to protect those who live there.

Cost: $$
Parts Used: Leaves
Associated Element: Fire
Magical Uses: Exorcism, hex-breaking, protection
Rituals and Celebrations: Banishing rituals
Substitutions: Hyssop, pennyroyal, or thistle
Often Used With: Amber, hematite, topaz
Applications: Use rue dipped in consecrated water to sprinkle around your home as a method of purification, or rub fresh leaves on your front door so that any hostile magic sent to you will be returned to the sender. Plant rue in the garden to protect your other herbs from pesky wildlife, or burn the dried leaves in an incense or as part of a smudging ritual to banish negativity.
Precautions: Rue can be toxic if ingested in large doses and should never be taken internally by pregnant women, as it can cause miscarriage.

Sage has been used for thousands of years; ancient priests burned dried sprigs in temples for religious rituals. The Greeks and Romans believed that inhaling the smoke imparted wisdom and mental acuity, and later Arab physicians said that sage brought about immortality. Sage is a multipurpose herb that comes in handy for purification and cleansing.

Cost: $
Parts Used: Essential oil, leaves
Associated Element: Air
Magical Uses: Cleansing and purification, mental acuity, psychic clarity, wisdom
Rituals and Celebrations: Lammas celebrations, smudging rituals
Blends Well With: Sweetgrass and rosemary for smudging
Substitutions: Sweetgrass
Often Used With: Amber, amethyst, selenite
Applications: Carry fresh sage leaves in your wallet or purse to promote financial gain. Burn the dried leaves to increase wisdom or gain guidance from spirit guides, bake it into bread or other dishes to bring about mental clarity, or smudge your home with sage for purification. If you want to make a wish come true, write your wish using sage oil on a piece of paper and then hide it beneath your pillow; if you dream about your wish over the next three nights, your desires will manifest!
Precautions: Sage essential oil should not be ingested by pregnant or nursing women, as the tannin content can cause breast milk to dry up.

SANDALWOOD *Santalum spicatum*

Although not truly an herb but a wood, sandalwood is an entire class of trees that are packed full of essential oils. Sandalwood oil is used in a number of rituals and spells, particularly related to cleansing and purification, and the wood and flowers can be utilized as well. Some species in the sandalwood family are endangered, but most of the sandalwood oil sold in the United States today is from the non-endangered Australian sandalwood. Use sandalwood in meditation and as a booster in other rituals.

Cost: $$$
Parts Used: Essential oil, flowers, wood
Associated Element: Water
Magical Uses: Grounding and stability, meditation, purification and cleansing
Rituals and Celebrations: Meditation, purification rituals
Blends Well With: Frankincense and myrrh for purification
Substitutions: Lavender
Often Used With: Carnelian, jet, smoky quartz
Applications: Use sandalwood oil to anoint and consecrate magical tools before ritual use, or burn the wood or flowers as incense to help with meditative journeys. Carry a bit of wood in your pocket if you have issues related to self-identity and trust, or dilute the oil in a base oil and sprinkle it around your home to keep your family bonds strong.
Precautions: Sandalwood is generally considered safe, but the essential oil should not be ingested for extended periods by anyone who is pregnant, is nursing, or suffers from kidney disease.

SUNFLOWER *Helianthus*

In many magical traditions, sunflowers are symbols of good luck. These bright, sunny blooms are also associated with truth, loyalty, and honesty. If you wish to have truth revealed to you, sleep with a sunflower under your pillow; the next day, the facts will become apparent. The sunflower is tied to fertility; to bring about conception, take a ritual bath with sunflower petals or wear a crown of sunflowers, particularly at Litha, the summer solstice. Sunflower oil has a mild flavor and scent, and can be used as a base oil.

Cost: $

Parts Used: Flowers, oil, seeds

Associated Element: Fire

Magical Uses: Fertility, good luck, loyalty, passion, truth

Rituals and Celebrations: Fertility rituals, Litha

Blends Well With: Lavender or lilac for love, cinnamon or mistletoe for fertility

Substitutions: Chamomile, heliotrope, marigold

Often Used With: Moonstone, selenite

Applications: Bake sunflower seeds or oil into a meal so that those who eat it will be honest and loyal to you. Plant sunflowers around your home to bring good fortune your way. When the flowers bloom, harvest the entire head of a sunflower and place it under your bed to give your sex life some extra heat.

Precautions: Sunflower oil can cause a reaction in those who are allergic to ragweed, marigolds, or chrysanthemums.

Sweetgrass is a popular herb for smudging and is used in a number of Native American ceremonies and rituals. Use it to call good spirits before starting a ritual or doing spellwork, or for smudging a sacred space.

Cost: $$$
Parts Used: Grass, leaves
Associated Element: Air
Magical Uses: Invoking positive energy, smudging
Rituals and Celebrations: Casting a circle, purification rituals
Blends Well With: Sage for purification
Substitutions: Rosemary, sage, vanilla
Often Used With: Garnet, selenite, topaz, turquoise
Applications: Use braided sweetgrass for smudging ceremonies or for calling positive energy into a sacred space. Hang sweetgrass in your home, or plant it near your door to invite good magic inside.
Precautions: Sweetgrass should not be ingested over long periods of time; it contains coumarin, which can cause hemorrhage and liver damage.

THISTLE *Cirsium vulgare*

Thistle comes in very handy for eliminating curses and negative magic. Stuff a doll with thistles to break a hex or spell that's been cast against you. Also an herb of vitality and power, thistle can be strewn around the house to boost the spirits and renew your energy levels. Carry dried thistle in a sachet for protection, or hang a bundle from the rafters to safeguard your home against lightning strikes.

Cost: $$

Parts Used: Flowers, leaves

Associated Element: Fire

Magical Uses: Hex-breaking, healing, strength and protection

Rituals and Celebrations: Autumn celebrations, healing rituals

Blends Well With: Holly for strength, yarrow for healing

Substitutions: Stinging nettle

Often Used With: Jet

Applications: Surround a black candle with dried thistles and burn it to eliminate hexes. If you suffer from nervous disorders or anxiety, place thistle in a sachet of blue cloth to bring about healing and calming energy. Powder a dried thistle and sprinkle it around your shoes to protect you as you travel to unfamiliar places.

Precautions: Thistle can secrete oils that cause irritation to sensitive skin; if you're handling fresh plants or the oils, be cautious.

Sir Walter Raleigh introduced tobacco to England in the late 1500s, and he made a small fortune in the tobacco market. In South America, indigenous groups used tobacco to help them communicate with spirits and to appease river gods when going on a trip over the water. Planting and growing your own tobacco isn't really feasible; it takes a long time and the plants take up a lot of space. When storing tobacco, you should always have a tin or pouch of it that you use only for magical reasons. If you're a smoker, never smoke the same tobacco you're using in ritual.

Cost: $$
Parts Used: Leaves
Associated Element: Fire
Magical Uses: Protection, purification, spirit communication
Rituals and Celebrations: Purification rituals, Samhain celebrations
Blends Well With: Comfrey or dandelion for spirit communication, sage or sweetgrass for cleansing or purification
Substitutions: Nearly any other magical herb
Often Used With: Hematite
Applications: Burn tobacco leaves in rituals, particularly divination, to call upon the spirit world. Sprinkle tobacco around your home to protect your family. If you suffer from nightmares, tuck tobacco leaves under your pillow at night.
Precautions: Tobacco is highly toxic and should not be taken internally. After you've used it in a ritual, be sure to wash your hands thoroughly.

VALERIAN *Valeriana wallichii*

Although it smells terrible—not unlike cat urine—valerian is a handy and useful magical herb. Hang it in your house to protect your home from fires, floods, or other natural disasters. Quarrels with family members can be resolved by placing sprigs of valerian leaves around the perimeter of the house and in the corners of your home. Hanging it over each door will keep discontent from entering the house. Also, despite its unpleasant aroma, many people swear by the use of valerian in love magic.

Cost: $$

Parts Used: Essential oil, leaves, roots

Associated Element: Water

Magical Uses: Love magic, peacemaking, protection

Rituals and Celebrations: Peace and tranquility

Blends Well With: Apple blossom and cinnamon for love magic, or basil and rosemary for protection

Substitutions: Patchouli, tobacco

Often Used With: Jet, obsidian

Applications: Carry a piece of valerian root in your pocket to protect you from hostile spirits or negative magic, or tuck a few leaves under your window to keep evil from entering. Hang a bundle in your home if you want to mend quarrels with the other people who live there.

Precautions: Short-term ingestion of valerian is considered reasonably safe, but over extended periods, it can cause digestive disorders, so caution is advised.

In the Middle Ages, yarrow was referred to as woundwort or knight's milfoil, because it was used in treatment of battle injuries and fever. It can also be incorporated into magical workings related to healing, love, and courage.

Cost: $$
Parts Used: Leaves
Associated Element: Water
Magical Uses: Courage, healing, passionate love, psychic development
Rituals and Celebrations: Healing rituals, Litha/summer solstice celebrations
Blends Well With: Mistletoe, peppermint, or thistle for healing; apple blossom, lavender, or lilac for love
Substitutions: Geranium, rose, rue
Often Used With: Emerald, rose quartz, tiger's eye
Applications: Carry yarrow in your pocket to boost your self-esteem or stop fear. Leaves strewn into a warm bath can help increase your psychic abilities, and yarrow can also be used to exorcise negative energies from a place or person. If you're working on a healing ritual for someone who is ill, burn dried yarrow as incense, or place it under the pillow to bring about restful, restorative sleep. A sprig hanging in the bedroom guarantees years of passionate love.
Precautions: Yarrow is highly toxic to dogs, cats, and horses, and can cause hyperventilation, vomiting, and diarrhea. If your pet ingests yarrow, call a vet immediately.

CHAPTER FOUR

Crystal Power

lthough their use is not unique to Wiccan practice, crystals
often play an important role in magical workings. They're
associated with aspects of the human experience, with gods
and goddesses, and with the power of ritual and ceremony.
In this chapter, we'll take a look at 20 of the crystals most commonly
used in Wiccan practice. This list is by no means comprehensive, but it is
more than enough to get you started. For a thorough list of resources on
crystals and their use, be sure to check the References section at the back
of the book.

Cleansing Your Crystals

Before you start working with crystals, it's important to be aware of
the different ways to care for them. Many people believe that, just like
any other magical tool, crystals should be cleansed before the first use.
This will eliminate any residual energies that the crystal has picked up
along its way prior to becoming yours and will allow you to start with a
clean slate.

There are several methods you can use for cleansing, but whichever
one you choose to work with is simply a matter of personal preference.
One of the most popular methods is to do a full ritual to cleanse and
purify your crystals; you can use the Tool Consecration Ritual in chapter 7 if you've got the time to do so.

Another easy way to cleanse crystals is to leave them out in a bowl
under the full moon overnight. In some magical traditions, crystals are

left out for three nights, starting the night before and ending the night after the moon's fullest phase. In other belief systems, they are left out during the waning moon phase as a way of eliminating negative energy.

Smudging is an effective way to clear negative energies. To do this, you can use smudge sticks made from sage, sweetgrass, other dried herbs, or even incense. When you light your herbal smudge stick, allow it to flame for a moment, and then blow it out to create a burning herb bundle. Pass your crystals through the smoke for cleansing.

Believe it or not, you may even want to bury your crystals. Place them in a bowl or jar, and completely cover them with dried herbs associated with cleansing, such as sage or sweetgrass, or soil from your own property. Alternatively, bury them directly in the ground; if you have an herb garden, it's the perfect spot to tuck crystals away for a night or two. You can also use stored consecrated water or running water, such as a river or creek, to cleanse them of negative energies.

Making your own consecrated water for ritual is easy! Place a cup of water outside on the night of the full moon, with a piece of silver dropped into it. Leave it outdoors overnight so the moonlight will bless the water, and then remove the silver in the morning. Store the water in a sealed bottle. You can also use seawater, which is considered naturally magical because it is a combination of water and salt. Keep in mind that while seawater is great for banishing rituals, it's not always useful for magic that brings things *to* you. That's because salt is associated with getting rid of things. It can, however, be used for purification magic.

Avoid using hot water for cleansing, as some crystals and stones can fracture or crack when immersed in it. In addition, porous stones can be damaged by sea salt, so skip using it unless you've done your homework to make sure your crystal won't be damaged.

Five Ways to Use Crystals in Magic

Depending on whom you ask, there are a number of different applications when it comes to using crystals in magic. You may soon find that you have a preferred method, and that's perfectly fine. Try a few of these techniques, and see what kind of magical results you can manifest.

Carry or Wear Your Crystal

Keep your crystals, whatever they may be, immediately available to you by carrying them in your pocket or wearing them as pieces of jewelry. If you're handy with a needle and thread, you can even sew them into your clothing. This allows you to attune yourself to the crystal's vibrations and help boost the magical connection you have with it.

Sleep with It at Night

Many crystals are useful in matters of intuition, wisdom, and dreamwork. These are stones you'll benefit from even more if you tuck them under your pillow or mattress. If the idea of a rock under your pillow makes you uncomfortable, leave it on the nightstand next to your side of the bed.

Crystal Elixirs

An elixir is simply water that has contained a crystal and has been magically consecrated. Place your crystal in a bowl of water, and leave it out in the moonlight to create an elixir; this allows the water to absorb the crystal's vibrations. Once you've removed the crystal the next day, use the water for magical purposes. This is especially useful with crystals related to healing magic, like carnelian.

Make a Crystal Grid

If you're using several crystals that have a similar purpose, such as healing or love, try placing them next to each other in a pattern to enhance each other's vibrations. Many people believe that sacred geometry can help open you up to the energy of the Divine and of the universe itself. To make a crystal grid, write your intention on a piece of paper, place it on your altar, and arrange crystals in a symmetrical, geometric pattern, like the pentagram, around the paper. Use this as a focal point of meditation in your magical working. For a number of specific crystal grid arrangements, check out the book *Crystals for Healing* by Karen Frazier or the website Crystalvaults.com. Searching Pinterest or other user-sourced websites will uncover helpful information, too.

Create Sacred Space

You may not have an entire room completely dedicated to meditation and spiritual endeavors, but with crystals, you can make any space sacred. Place your crystals, particularly those related to spiritual growth and development, in the area of your home in which you meditate. Hold them in both hands as you meditate, and take advantage of their vibrations to both calm you and help you connect to a higher power.

> "Choosing a crystal is unique to each individual, because crystals may vibrate differently with different people's energy. Be sure to pay close attention to your inner voice when choosing a crystal. Making a selection that feels good to you is an intuitive process."
>
> —Karen Frazier, *Crystals for Healing: The Complete Reference Guide*

AGATE

Agate is a brown, gold, or green stone, sometimes found with bands across it. It's related to matters of the mind. Use it in workings related to energy, depression, and mental health. Agate is particularly useful in rituals for overcoming feelings of loneliness or sadness, moving past hurtful memories, and truth and self-discovery.

Associated Element: Earth
Magical Uses: Energy booster, mental health
Rituals and Celebrations: Healing magic, Ostara, rituals for new beginnings
Often Used With: Feverfew, hyssop, peppermint, selenite, smoky quartz
Applications: Carry an agate in your pocket when you're feeling sad or lonely, or if you feel as though stress is beginning to get the best of you. When you go to sleep, place an agate beneath your pillow to help give your energy levels a boost during waking hours. Feeling emotionally drained? Wear a piece of agate jewelry to lift your spirits.
Associated Colors: Blue, brown, gold, green

Amber isn't technically a gemstone or crystal but a resin formed by hardened tree sap; it often contains impurities such as fossilized insects or bits of plant detritus. It's worth including here, though, because magically it functions in the same way crystals do. Although it's found primarily in the Baltic Sea region, amber has been discovered in most parts of the world. You can use it for workings involving communication, mental clarity, and strength. Because of the physical properties of amber, avoid using salt or water for cleansing; either of these can cause damage to the piece.

Associated Element: Fire
Magical Uses: Clarity, communication, confidence, protection, strength
Rituals and Celebrations: Lammas
Often Used With: Chamomile, rose quartz, rue, sage
Applications: Carry amber if you wish to communicate effectively on a professional level. If you're hoping someone else will call or contact you, place amber near your phone—carry it in the same pocket as your cell phone! Place it at your desk to protect yourself from malicious workplace gossip. Hold a piece in your hands while you meditate, to clear your mind of unnecessary clutter and help boost your mood.
Associated Colors: Orange, yellow

Amethyst is a form of quartz and appears in a wide range of purple and violet colors. Use amethyst in healing rituals related to mood disorders, such as anxiety, addiction, or depression. On a magical level, amethyst comes in handy for clarity of mind and enhancement of your psychic gifts, as well as for cleansing of sacred space.

Associated Element: Water

Magical Uses: Addiction, cleansing, mental health, psychic development

Rituals and Celebrations: Imbolc, Mabon

Often Used With: Amber, chamomile, lavender, sage, smoky quartz

Applications: Carry amethyst with you if you're going out for a social event or to help keep you from overindulging; the ancient Greeks used it to avoid drunkenness. If you've got a meditation space in your home, place amethysts around the area where you normally sit to aid in clearing your mind and facilitating a connection to the Divine. Do you experience general anxiety? A piece of amethyst jewelry can be calming. Place a stone on your nightstand or under your pillow to bring about restful sleep.

Associated Colors: Lavender, purple

BLOODSTONE

Bloodstone, or heliotrope, is a green speckled stone that typically includes shades of red and gold, and is related to both the planet Mars and the sun. Use bloodstone in magical workings related to fertility, prosperity, and intuition. Bloodstone is especially useful in matters of passion and wisdom.

Associated Element: Fire

Magical Uses: Abundance, fertility, prosperity

Rituals and Celebrations: Beltane, Imbolc, Yule

Often Used With: Apple blossom, aventurine, basil, cinnamon, garnet, citrine, mugwort

Applications: Place a bloodstone under your bed if you're trying to conceive; carry it with you to doctors' appointments to rule out medical causes of infertility. Wear bloodstone jewelry to attract passionate love. Draw abundance and prosperity to you by tucking a bloodstone into your purse or wallet, or place one in the cash register or safe at work if you own a business. To develop intuition and wisdom, tap into bloodstone's solar energy, and hold a piece in your hands while you meditate on a bright, sunny day.

Associated Colors: Green, gold, red

Although mostly red and orange, carnelian is often streaked with white. The healing powers of carnelian are associated with impotence and infertility. Use carnelian in grounding rituals, because of its connection to the element of Earth. In addition to grounding, carnelian is useful in shielding against psychic attack.

Associated Element: Earth
Magical Uses: Grounding, sexual energy and fertility, shielding
Rituals and Celebrations: Beltane
Often Used With: Apple blossom, clear quartz, dandelion, hematite, mandrake, selenite, sandalwood
Applications: Keep carnelian with your other crystals to help shield them from negative energy; think of it as a magical protective barrier. Wear it in a ring or other piece of jewelry to prevent jealousy and envy from getting out of control. Make healing water by immersing a carnelian stone in consecrated water overnight under a full moon; use this as a cleansing wash or to sprinkle around a sickroom. Place carnelian at the four corners of your bed to boost sexual potency.
Associated Colors: Orange, red

The diamonds you're accustomed to seeing in engagement rings are polished, cut, and sparkly, and are typically associated with love and marriage. However, uncut diamonds look very different; uncut, they are usually gray, yellow, white, or even pink, and often small and lumpy. With a strong link to the sun, diamonds can be used in workings related to astral travel, scrying, and intuitive power.

Associated Elements: Air, Fire

Magical Uses: Astral travel, fidelity, love, intuition, marriage, personal power

Rituals and Celebrations: Handfastings, Lammas, Litha

Often Used With: Basil, citrine, comfrey, garnet, mugwort, rose quartz

Applications: You can wear diamonds to ensure fidelity in relationships, or use them in meditation if you're trying to make a decision about your love life. Attract new love into your life by keeping a diamond close to your heart; this will also help in developing love for self.

Associated Colors: Gray, pink, white, yellow

The emerald is lush and green, and can be used to lift the spirit and calm the mind when you're feeling emotionally vulnerable. Considered a sacred stone of eternal life, emeralds were used by the Egyptians and Greeks as talismans for both love magic and financial fortune. Use emeralds to revive lost passion and restore confidence and self-esteem, or even to boost business in times of economic downturn.

Associated Element: Earth

Magical Uses: Calming anxiety, confidence, love, money, passion

Rituals and Celebrations: Litha, love spells

Often Used With: Aventurine, basil, catnip, cinnamon, citrine, goldenseal, lilac, yarrow

Applications: Carry an emerald in your pocket, or wear it close to your heart to attract long-term love and passionate romance. An emerald held in the hands during meditation can calm an agitated, busy mind. Place one under your pillow at bedtime; if you dream of emeralds in your sleep, it's a sign of prosperity and worldly success, particularly if you own a business.

Associated Colors: Green

Garnets appear most commonly in shades of red and purple, although they can occasionally show up in other colors like green, gold, and orange. Some people believe that a garnet obtained through theft or deception will bring a curse upon the person who has it until the person makes things right with the original owner, so don't steal a garnet! In terms of magic, garnet is connected to moon magic, and subsequently to intuition and women's mysteries. Use it in rituals for balance (especially between the spiritual and the physical) or to enhance the energies of other crystals in magical workings.

Associated Element: Fire
Magical Uses: Balance, moon magic, intuition, passion, women's mysteries
Rituals and Celebrations: Full moon rituals, Imbolc, Lammas
Often Used With: Aventurine, bloodstone, cinnamon, lemon balm, mugwort, sweetgrass
Applications: Garnet can be carried in your pocket or worn in a piece of jewelry to develop your personal power and bring balance between the spiritual and physical planes. Use it during lunar rituals to promote intuitive abilities and psychic skills. Keep a garnet in your meditation area to give other crystals a boost while keeping negative energy at bay.
Associated Colors: Green, gold, orange, purple, red

HEMATITE

Hematite is an extremely popular crystal to use in magic, but the shiny silver stones you're used to seeing look that way only because they've been smoothed and polished. In its raw form, hematite is a deep rust color and is sometimes referred to as paint ore or iron rose. Associated with the planet Saturn as well as the sun, hematite can be used in healing rituals and protective magic, as well as for developing confidence, problem-solving skills, psychic clarity, and willpower.

Associated Element: Fire
Magical Uses: Confidence and courage, healing, protection, psychic awareness
Rituals and Celebrations: Mabon, protection rituals, Samhain
Often Used With: Chamomile, feverfew, holly, lemon balm, obsidian, onyx, rue, tobacco leaf
Applications: Place hematite at the four corners of your property to protect yourself from those who might want to cause you physical harm. Carry a piece in your pocket or tuck it in your car's glove compartment to stay safe when traveling. If you have a meditation space, hematite placed at the doors and windows will help prevent psychic attack. Hematite also helps dissipate negative energies, so if you're sensitive to being bombarded with information and emotions when you're in a crowd, wear a piece of hematite jewelry.
Associated Colors: Deep red, silver

Found all over the world, jasper is a stone that typically appears in a brownish red color, but it can also be green, white, or yellow. Jasper is great for healing magic, especially related to chronic illness. It's also perfect for grounding and centering after a ritual, and can provide stability and balance to relationships. Use red jasper to give your passion a boost, and get a little extra spark in your sex life!

Associated Element: Earth
Magical Uses: Centering, grounding, healing, passion, stability
Rituals and Celebrations: Healing rituals, Yule
Often Used With: Carnelian, cinnamon, feverfew, mandrake, patchouli, smoky quartz
Applications: Place jasper beneath your mattress for an extra-enthusiastic sex life. Use in grounding rituals after magical workings to get yourself centered and refocused. If you're doing healing magic, place jasper anywhere on the body that is affected by illness or injury. Cleanse jasper by placing it in a bowl with a piece of hematite.
Associated Colors: Brown, green, red, white, yellow

Unlike many of the other stones used in magic, jet is actually fossilized Jurassic-era driftwood that has transformed into lignite coal. It comes in very handy in talismans and jewelry because it can be polished to a mirror-like sheen. The energy of jet can be used to purify and protect, and jet is often associated with grief; the Victorians used it to make mourning brooches and rosaries. Today, you can use jet to protect against evil and psychic attacks.

Associated Element: Earth
Magical Uses: Absorbing negativity, grief, grounding, protection
Rituals and Celebrations: Banishing rituals, funerals, Samhain
Often Used With: Amber, chamomile, holly, lavender, onyx, obsidian, pennyroyal, rosemary, sandalwood, thistle, valerian
Applications: Wear a necklace or brooch of jet to aid in healing from grief and mourning. It can also be used to dispel negative energy. Keep a piece handy to prevent psychic attack and emotional possession or addiction. If someone is harassing you and you want to get them out of your life, write or scratch the person's name on a piece of jet and throw it in a running stream or river. From your bedpost, hang a piece of jet alongside amber to ensure a restful sleep without nightmares.
Associated Colors: Black

A lodestone is naturally magnetic—literally and spiritually. This quality makes lodestone useful when it comes to spellwork, and you don't need a large piece to work effective magic. Lodestone attracts iron, such as nails and pins, but you can also "feed" it with magnetic sand or iron shavings. Often used in love magic and for workings related to money and prosperity, lodestone can also be utilized as a natural compass representing all four directions. Don't use water to cleanse a lodestone, as this will cause it to rust. Instead, leave it out in the moonlight for three nights.

Associated Element: Water

Magical Uses: Attraction, love, money

Rituals and Celebrations: Any rituals involving attraction

Often Used With: Aventurine, citrine, goldenseal

Applications: Write a list of goals, and place a lodestone on top of it. Feed your lodestone with metal shavings representing the dreams you hope to realize. In some traditions of folk magic, lodestones are paired up as "male" and "female." If you can find a set of these, use them in love magic to draw a partner to you or keep your current partner close. Attract financial abundance by dressing a lodestone with Money Oil (see page 126) and sprinkling it with fine metal shavings.

Associated Colors: Black, dark green

Moonstone, considered sacred in India, gets its name from its appearance. It's a polished stone that often looks like a reflection of the moon's surface. As such, it's often associated with lunar deities, particularly goddesses with triple aspects. You can use moonstone in workings related to female reproduction and childbirth, as well as for wisdom and intuition, women's mysteries, and ceremonies honoring the sacred feminine.

Associated Element: Water

Magical Uses: Female energy, moon magic, wisdom and intuition

Rituals and Celebrations: Moon rituals

Often Used With: Clear quartz, garnet, mugwort, selenite, sunflower

Applications: Put moonstone under the bed of a woman in labor to help aid in a smooth and healthy childbirth, or place it anywhere on the body that needs general healing energy. Do a ritual honoring lunar goddesses and leave your moonstone out overnight, under the moonlight, in a bowl of water. Use this healing water as a skin wash or to sprinkle around a sickroom. If you're feeling jittery and off-kilter, carrying moonstone in your pocket or wearing it as jewelry will help your body's natural rhythms become better attuned. Pair a piece of moonstone with a garnet to reveal the truth about a matter that has been hidden from you.

Associated Colors: Gray, peach, silver, white

Obsidian is actually volcanic glass, and it can appear clear and smooth or have sharp, raw edges. Use obsidian for workings involving developing intuition and dreamwork, removing negativity, or scrying. Obsidian is effective in magic relating to shedding baggage or ending toxic attachments and habits; it's also known as a stone that can be used to protect those who are sensitive and gentle from emotional harm. Green obsidian can deflect psychic energies that might otherwise leave you feeling drained, as does snowflake obsidian.

Associated Element: Fire

Magical Uses: Banishing, dreamwork, intuition, magical shielding, scrying

Rituals and Celebrations: Samhain, scrying rituals

Often Used With: Chamomile, comfrey, lilac, jet, onyx, pennyroyal, valerian, white quartz

Applications: Carry obsidian to keep you grounded during protection and shielding rituals. Tuck a piece under your pillow at bedtime to aid in lucid dreaming; before you fall asleep, focus on any questions that must be answered, and the solution should appear to you in your dreams. If you need to banish someone from your life, write the individual's name on a piece of obsidian, and throw it into a moving body of water. If you can find a ball or sphere made of obsidian, use it for divination work and scrying. To regain balance in your life, pair obsidian with a similarly sized piece of white quartz. Cleanse obsidian by placing it in any sort of natural light, whether from the moon or the sun.

Associated Colors: Black, green, white

Onyx typically appears in black, although you may sometimes encounter it with white bands or spots. Like other black stones, onyx absorbs negativity, so it's useful for protection. It can provide emotional strength during times of trouble and help eliminate unwanted energies or feelings. Use onyx for workings related to increasing your own willpower or self-control.

Associated Element: Fire
Magical Uses: Banishing, protection, strength, willpower
Rituals and Celebrations: Imbolc, Samhain
Often Used With: Chamomile, hematite, holly, jet, lilac, obsidian, pennyroyal
Applications: Carry a piece of onyx in your pocket or place stones around the corners of your home and property to keep away those who would cause you harm. If you're struggling with addiction, obsession, or impulse control, wear onyx as a pendant. If there's someone in your life whose habits or poor decision-making skills have negative consequences, write the person's name on a piece of paper, wrap it around a piece of onyx, and bury it in the ground during the waning moon phase.
Associated Colors: Black, white

Quartz appears in a variety of shapes and colors, and is a versatile crystal in metaphysical practices. Clear or white quartz is connected to all four elements and can be used for healing rituals or the enhancement of intuition and spiritual growth. Rose quartz is often associated with love and relationships, as well as relief of emotional issues and drama. Smoky gray quartz can be used for grounding and centering, as well as for absorbing negative energies.

Associated Element: All (clear), Earth (smoky), Water (rose)

Magical Uses: Grounding and stability (smoky), healing and intuition (clear), love and friendship (rose)

Rituals and Celebrations: Healing rituals, Ostara

Often Used With: Amber, jet, lemon balm, mugwort (clear); amber, mandrake, sandalwood, tiger's eye (smoky); garnet, lilac, moonstone, yarrow (rose)

Applications: Place clear quartz in a bowl with other crystals to amplify their energies. Use it in general healing magic by placing it on the parts of the body affected by illness or injury. Clear quartz also provides protection from negativity.

Rose quartz can be used to boost self-esteem and draw romance and friendship your way. Hold a piece of rose quartz during meditation to help heal from childhood trauma, emotional abuse, or feelings of abandonment.

To develop confidence and self-esteem, carry smoky quartz with you. Place a piece near your mirror to bring about feelings of calmness and inner beauty.

Associated Colors: Brown, clear, gray, pink, white

SELENITE

Selenite gets its name from Selene, the moon goddess, and is associated with angel magic, enlightenment, emotion, and inspiration and creativity. It is a stone of truth and honesty, and can be used to help with decision making and with opening your mind to new opinions and ideas. Because selenite is a type of gypsum, it is easily scratched or damaged. Use care when working with it. Don't use salt or water for cleansing because either one will ruin the stone.

Associated Element: Water
Magical Uses: Angels, creativity, decision making, enlightenment, inspiration
Rituals and Celebrations: Moon rituals, Yule
Often Used With: Moonstone, sage, sunflower, sweetgrass
Applications: Keep selenite rods or towers in your meditation area to facilitate communication between you and the Divine, as well as to purify the energy of the space. Carry a piece in your pocket or wear it as jewelry if you're worried about losing inspiration or your creative muse. If you believe in angels, try sleeping with selenite under your pillow to receive angelic messages in your dreams. Include selenite in a spell to attract someone who is enlightened and spiritually aware.
Associated Colors: White

The Shiva Lingam stone is prevalent in many aspects of Hindu belief and is a symbol of the Hindu god Shiva. Shaped a bit like an elongated egg, the Shiva Lingam comes in a variety of sizes, ranging from less than half an inch to several feet long. Each stone's markings are unique, and the stone symbolizes Divine creation and the sacred balance of the soul. Because of its shape and similarity to phallic symbolism, the Shiva Lingam is often associated with male and female aspects of life, as well as potency, sexual fertility, and whole-self healing.

Associated Element: All

Magical Uses: Fertility and potency, healing

Rituals and Celebrations: Beltane, fertility rituals

Often Used With: Apple blossom, carnelian, dandelion, mandrake, mistletoe, moss agate, patchouli

Applications: Place Shiva Lingam in a charm bag with other fertility stones like moss agate and carnelian. Keep this under your bed to help improve your chances of conceiving a child. If there's a man in your life who's suffering from impotence or a lack of sexual desire, place a Shiva Lingam stone in a jar of water in the sunlight; sprinkle the water around his side of the bed, or use it in a wash before lovemaking.

Associated Colors: Brown, gray, red

The tiger's eye stone gets its name from its brownish-tan or gold colors with black banding. Tiger's eye can be used to enhance overall energy and general physical health, as well as in rituals related to self-confidence, courage, and inner strength. If you need to see something clearly before making a decision, incorporate tiger's eye.

Associated Element: Fire
Magical Uses: Clarity, healing, self-confidence, strength
Rituals and Celebrations: Litha
Often Used With: Amethyst, catnip, cinnamon, feverfew, hematite, peppermint, yarrow
Applications: Wear a tiger's eye pendant to help boost your courage and confidence when you're walking into new, unfamiliar situations. Carry a piece in your pocket along with amethyst and hematite to filter out the negative energy of those who might try to sabotage your success. To give your tiger's eye a bit of additional power, place it outside in the afternoon sun for a few hours, but bring it in before dusk.
Associated Colors: Brown, gold, yellow

Like quartz, topaz can be found in several colors, but it generally appears in yellow or blue. Use yellow topaz to bring success and good fortune, as well as to protect yourself from greed. The blue variety is calming and brings about inner peace, spiritual love, and creativity; it can also enhance your leadership abilities. Pink comes in handy when it comes to matters of the mind, such as studying and memory.

Associated Element: Fire

Magical Uses: Abundance, calming, meditation, protection from greed, success

Rituals and Celebrations: Mabon, meditation rituals

Often Used With: Catnip, holly, moonstone, rosemary, rue, sweetgrass, turquoise

Applications: Combine yellow topaz with moonstone and turquoise for success in business; place all three stones in a pouch and keep it tucked away at your workstation. Carry blue topaz to calm yourself down, especially if you're about to walk into a situation where you have to demonstrate your leadership. Got a big test coming up? Keep a pink topaz near your study resources, and then place it under your pillow the night before the test. This will help you retain the information you've read.

Associated Colors: Blue, pink, yellow

Turquoise is perhaps best known for its use in the artwork and jewelry of the Native American people of the Southwest, but it is found all over the world, including in Tibet and Egypt. It appears in various shades of blue, from light to dark, and often appears speckled or banded with black or white streaks. Use turquoise in rituals to bring about wisdom and intuition, and to seek connection between the natural and Divine.

Associated Element: Water

Magical Uses: Intuition, spiritual development, wisdom

Rituals and Celebrations: Imbolc

Often Used With: Agate, amethyst, mugwort, sweetgrass

Applications: Give a turquoise stone to a new friend to show mutual generosity or to bring financial success and abundance toward your friend. Carry one in your pocket to aid in decision making, especially if you have to choose between two equally appealing options. Keep turquoise in your meditation area to aid in spiritual growth and development, as well as your connection to the deities. If you need to promote marital harmony, both partners should wear a piece of turquoise jewelry.

Associated Colors: Blue, green

PART III

Living Practice

"I wash away negativity, opening myself up to light and love and all things good and beneficial."

—Deborah Blake, *Everyday Witchcraft: Making Time for Spirit in a Too-Busy World*

We've talked about many of the useful herbs, oils, and crystals for magical practice. Now it's time to bring them all together. In part 3, we'll look at basic spells for daily life, as well as some simple meditations and rituals for various life milestones and seasonal markers. You can think of the spellcrafts as being similar to recipes in a cookbook. When you perform a spell, meditation, or ritual, you can certainly use it as is. As you become more proficient, feel free to experiment with each, trying your own modifications just as you would with a recipe.

CHAPTER FIVE
Everyday Spells

I n this chapter, we'll work through 30 simple spells that you can use as part of your day-to-day magical practice. Some of these are workings you won't need very often; after all, once you've brought romantic love into your life, ideally you won't need to do it again. Others, such as money spells, can be repeated as often as needed. Find the ones that work best for you, and make some life-changing magic! Each spell is labeled by its purpose, as listed below.

Protection Spells

Protection workings are a very useful application of your magical knowledge. Use these simple spells to keep yourself, your family, and your home safe from negative influences, both mundane and metaphysical.

Love Spells

Love magic has been a focus of spellwork for thousands of years. The ancient Greeks and Romans left records of love spells in various forms. In some magical traditions, it is believed that to perform a love spell is to infringe upon the free will of another person. If you feel that way but still want to use magic to bring love into your life, you can instead do it to open yourself up to new love, without a specific individual in mind, or to develop self-love, which can certainly enhance the way you are seen by others.

Money Magic

While magic may not help you win the lottery—after all, the odds are stacked against you—it can definitely help you add a little bit to your wallet as you need it. Try these simple spells to give your bank account a boost.

Healing Magic

When you or a loved one is ill or injured, it's natural to want to improve things with magic. Healing energy can be used to aid with anxiety and stress, bring about restful and calming sleep, bring about general health and wellness, or provide pain relief. It's important to note, however, that magic should not be used as a substitute for professional medical care and should only be used alongside it to lend assistance. In other words, see a doctor in addition to working healing magic.

Banishing Spells

Sometimes, you've just got to get rid of something. Whether it's another person who won't leave you alone, a pesky entity that's hanging around your house, or just an overall feeling of negativity, banishing can be very useful indeed. While some see banishing as manipulative magic on the theory that it impinges on the free will of another, you are the only one who can decide if banishing is acceptable to you.

Binding Magic

If banishing magic is used to eliminate something, binding magic is used to restrict it. In general, a magical binding is simply a spell that restrains someone and prevents the person from doing something. It is often used to keep people from harming themselves or others.

Luck Magic

Everyone wants to feel lucky, and there are certain herbs and crystals that can be utilized in good-luck magic. Take advantage of them, and use them to bring good fortune your way.

Crystal Home Protection Charm

If you want to keep your home safe, a great way to do so is by using crystals in a simple charm packet. In addition to using protective stones, you can use a drawing or photo of your home to create a magical link to the house. Gather:

A photograph or illustration of your home
1 piece of amber
1 piece of carnelian
4 pieces of hematite
1 foot of yellow ribbon or yarn

1. Go outside on a sunny day. Place the photo of your home in front of you, and focus on the image. Visualize warm, protective solar energy flowing around the house, through the doors and windows and filling the entire home. Hold the amber between your hands. Say, *"Power of the sun, fill this home with warmth and light. Protect this home with warmth and light."* Then, place the amber in the center of the photo.

2. Hold the carnelian in your hands, and say, *"Power of the earth, make this home safe and stable. Let all who dwell here know they are safe and stable."* Next, place the carnelian in the center of the photo, and place the hematite stones on the photo so they are lined up with the four cardinal directions. Say, *"Earth, Air, Fire, Water, I call upon all the magic of all four elements to pro-tect this home. No matter which way we may turn, no matter which direction we face, this house is a home of love, safety, and understanding. All those who live within will be well."* After you've recited these words, move the hematite stones into the center with the amber and carnelian, and fold the photo as many times as you can so that the stones are contained within a paper packet. Use the yellow ribbon to tie the packet shut, and bury the package in your yard near the front door.

Protection Incense Spell

The use of incense and its smoke is one of the oldest forms of magic, long predating Wicca. You can certainly purchase incense prepackaged in cones and sticks, but loose-leaf incense has the same effect and allows the option of customizing your blend. To use it, you'll need one of the charcoal discs specifically designed for incense burning; do not use barbecue charcoal. Combine protective herbs together to create this loose incense, and use the smoke to provide protection for people and objects. Gather:

2 bay leaves, crushed

2 teaspoons dried basil

2 teaspoons dried sage

1 teaspoon dried thistle

1 teaspoon dried valerian

2 drops sandalwood essential oil

1 charcoal incense disc

1. Combine the herbs and the sandalwood oil in a bowl, mixing them thoroughly.

2. Light the charcoal disc by carefully holding a match to it; the disc will probably spark when you first light it, so be sure to place it in a fireproof bowl or brazier.

3. Add 1 teaspoon of the loose incense blend; you can store the rest for later use. Once the incense has begun to smoke, you can use it to smudge anything that needs protection, such as personal belongings or vehicles. Pass the items through the smoke, speaking the words, *"I protect you from evil; I protect you from harm; I protect you from damage; I protect you from theft. I claim this item as mine, and it is protected by my will."* When you're finished, allow the incense to burn out on its own.

Protection Oil

To blend a batch of this oil, use herbs that are associated with protection magic. By combining them together in a base oil and working with a yellow candle—the color associated with protection—you'll be able to craft an oil blend that you can use to keep yourself and your loved ones safe. Gather:

A yellow candle
2 ounces base oil, such as grapeseed, jojoba, or sunflower
1 fresh basil leaf, chopped
1 small pinch dried catnip
2 drops cinnamon essential oil
4 drops sandalwood essential oil

1. Find a quiet place to work, and begin by lighting the yellow candle. Pour your base oil into a bowl, and slowly add the basil, catnip, cinnamon oil, and sandalwood oil. Swirl the bowl slowly in a clockwise direction to blend your ingredients, speaking the words, *"Safe and sound, safe from harm, safe from those who would do me wrong. Draw protection here to me, as I will, so it shall be."*

2. Use your protection oil to anoint the doors and windows of your home to keep negative energy and harmful people away from you and your loved ones. Store your oil in a dark-colored bottle, and replenish as needed.

Protection Seasoning

So much magic can take place in the kitchen; it is, after all, the center of activity in many homes. If you're doing meal prep regularly, incorporate magic into your cooking process. Blend up this seasoning to use in savory dishes to give all your guests a little extra layer of magic protection. Gather:

1 bay leaf, crushed

2 teaspoons dried basil

2 teaspoons dried sage

1 teaspoon dried onion

1 teaspoon garlic powder

½ teaspoon dried dill

½ teaspoon sea salt

¼ teaspoon black pepper

In a bowl, blend all your ingredients, stirring in a clockwise direction. If you have a mortar and pestle, use it—this is a great way to help release the flavors of the herbs in this seasoning blend. As you mix them, say, "A taste of hospitality, a taste of protection, a taste of safety for all those who sit at my table. Blessings to my family, blessings to my guests, blessings to any who dine with me. May they be safe and healthy." When you add this seasoning to your meals, a teaspoon or two at a time, repeat the incantation as you stir it into the dish. Store your seasoning in a sealed jar until you're ready to use it.

Spell for Protection from Negativity

In addition to physical protection, you can also do magical workings to protect yourself from metaphysical danger. If you think someone is sending hostile magic your way, or if there's a sense of negative energy surrounding you, use this spell to push it out of your life. Perform this spell during the waning moon phase. Gather:

A small bowl of water
1 tablespoon sea salt
1 tablespoon dried sage

1. Sit outside so the moonlight is reflected in the bowl of water. Close your eyes, and imagine the moon's calming, soft energy flowing around you, like a protective cloak. Speak the words, *"As the moon wanes and fades away, I send with it the negative energy that surrounds me."* Next, sprinkle the salt into the water, use your finger to stir it in a counterclockwise direction, and say, *"As this salt purifies the water, I purify all that surrounds me so that I may be enveloped in positive energy."*

2. Then, add the sage, stirring once more. Say, *"As this sage cleanses the water, so I cleanse the energy around me, sending negativity far away."* Finally, hold the bowl up to the moonlight. Speak the words, *"As the moon wanes and fades away, I send with it the negative energy that surrounds me. I will be cloaked in love and light, and that which could do me harm has power no longer."* Leave the bowl out for three nights. Afterward, pour the water into a bottle with a lid for safekeeping. Dab a bit on your wrists and the soles of your feet each day until the danger has passed.

Threshold Blessing Spell

Many Wiccans maintain their homes as sacred space at all times. This is a helpful strategy because it allows you to control what sort of energy comes and goes. In addition, doing a preventive threshold blessing spell before anything bad happens can alleviate the need to do bigger magical workings later. Do this working on a bright, sunny day. Gather:

2 gallons warm water
8 cups fresh lemon balm leaves
9 drops lavender essential oil
A new sponge or washcloth

Add the lemon balm and lavender oil to the warm water and mix thoroughly. Dip the sponge or washcloth in the warm water, and use it to wash down your front door's threshold and frame, starting at the doorknob and working in a clockwise direction. As you do so, chant, *"Home and hearth, hearth and home, this sacred space I call my own. Blessed by love, never in doubt, good stays within, and bad without."* When you're done, pour the remainder of the water out across your front walkway that leads up to the door. Refresh this blessing every three months as the seasons change.

Candle Magic for a Lucky Love Life

Some people truly believe that they're unlucky in love. While it's possible that this is the case, it's also true that other people tend to view us the way we view ourselves. In other words, if you truly feel as though you'll never meet the right person, it could be a self-fulfilling prophecy. Use a bit of candle magic to improve your love for self and open yourself up to new romantic possibilities. Gather:

A pink candle
3 drops New Romance Oil (page 122)
1 tablespoon powdered ginger

Use your fingers to gently rub the oil onto the candle, and then roll the candle in the ginger, which is associated with confidence. Light the candle, speaking the words, *"I am worthy of love, I am worthy of passion, I am worthy of romance. I have so much to give, so much to offer, so much to share. I am a person of value, I am entitled to find someone who deserves me, and I will deserve him or her in return. I am worthy of love, and I call it into my life."* Meditate on the candle flame for a while, and as you watch it, visualize feelings of love radiating outward from you, to let others know you are receptive to romance. Allow the candle to burn out on its own.

Herb Spell for Long-Distance Love

Sometimes, for a variety of reasons, we find ourselves in relationships with people who live far away. While long-distance love presents a unique set of challenges, it's often manageable with a little bit of work on the part of both parties. Of course, a bit of herbal magic helps as well! You'll need your partner's assistance to complete this working, so, if possible, you should do it prior to being parted. Gather:

2 stamped envelopes
A pink pen or crayon
2 small pieces of pink paper
½ cup dried chamomile flowers
1 tablespoon dried lavender
2 teaspoons dried peppermint

1. On the inside flaps of both envelopes, use the pink pen or crayon to write your name and your lover's name entwined in a heart. On one piece of paper, write your name, and on the other, your partner's.

2. Blend the herbs together in a bowl, and pour equal amounts onto each of the two pieces of paper. Fold the papers up carefully so that the herbs don't fall out, and then place one piece of paper in each envelope. Seal the envelopes.

3. Mail the one with your name inside it to your partner, and ask your partner to mail the one with their name inside to you. When the envelopes arrive in the mail, neither of you should open them; instead, place them someplace safe until the two of you are reunited again.

Love Magic Dolls

The use of dolls in magic is fairly widespread throughout different cultures. A magical doll can be made out of any material, such as clay or wax, but the most common method is to stitch one out of fabric. Don't worry if you're not too handy with a needle and thread; this is fairly basic stitching that anyone can do with a little effort. If you know the type of person you'd like to attract, make a doll to represent their various appealing qualities, and one to represent yourself. If possible, do this spell during the waxing moon phase. Gather:

¼ yard felt, cotton, or muslin

A needle, thread, and scissors

2 teaspoons dried lemon balm

2 teaspoons dried patchouli

2 drops rose essential oil

Cotton or synthetic stuffing

12 inches of pink ribbon

1. Cut out four identical shapes from the fabric to make your dolls—two pieces to represent each of you. The easiest shape to work with is that of a gingerbread person; it has a head, arms, legs, and a body.

2. Place two of the doll shapes together, with the right sides facing each other, and begin stitching around the edge. As you do so, imagine yourself welcoming love, warmth, and romance into your life. Think about all the wonderful gifts you have to offer a new significant other. When you have only a couple of inches left to sew, stop so you have an opening in the doll, and turn it right side out.

3. Do the same thing with the other two pieces, which will represent the lover you wish to attract. As you sew, think about all the characteristics you want to see in a partner. Do you want someone with a sense of humor? An intellectual type? Perhaps you seek someone with a sense of adventure. Visualize all these attributes. When you have enough space left for an opening, stop stitching, and turn the doll right side out.

4. Blend the lemon balm, patchouli, and rose oil together in a bowl, stirring gently in a clockwise direction and visualizing what an ideal relationship would be for you. Use a spoon or your fingers to place equal amounts of the herb blend into each doll, and then fill them the rest of the way with the stuffing. Stitch the openings closed, again thinking about your own good qualities and those of a future partner.

5. When you have finished, use the pink ribbon to tie the dolls together so they are holding hands. As you tie the dolls together, speak the words, *"Equal love, equal measure, I call to me someone to treasure. I open my heart to love today, and call a new romance my way."* Place the dolls under your bed until new love has come into your life.

Love Magic Mojo Bag

If you want to attract romance into your life, it helps to just put the fact that you're looking for love out into the universe. Send a metaphysical message by crafting a Love Magic Mojo Bag to wear or carry in your pocket when you go out to socialize. Gather:

½ teaspoon dried apple blossom
½ teaspoon ground cinnamon
½ teaspoon dried patchouli
½ teaspoon dried yarrow
4-x-5-inch square of pink cloth
30 inches of red ribbon

Blend the herbs together, and as you do, recite the words, *"I give love, I receive love, I attract love here to me. I draw respect, I draw fidelity, I draw passion, and I draw romance."* Place the herbs on the center of the cloth square. Carefully draw the edges together, and tie the square shut with the ribbon. Knot the ends of the ribbon together so that you can hang the bag around your neck. Be sure to tuck it into your shirt so it stays close to your heart.

Loyal Lover Honey Spell

If you want to keep your lover loyal and faithful to you, a bit of magic can help promote relationship harmony. Use crystals and herbs associated with truth and fidelity to help ensure that your partner will stay by your side and not go wandering elsewhere, and include a bit of honey to sweeten the deal. Gather:

A glass jar with a lid
A copy of a photo of you and your lover together
2 pieces of amber
2 pieces of rose quartz
2 pieces of turquoise
1 cup raw honey (or enough to cover the photo and the crystals)

1. Place the photo of you and your lover in the bottom of the jar, facing upward. Drop the pieces of amber on top of the photo, speaking the words, *"Amber for loyalty, fidelity, and a constant heart, one for you, and one for me."* Drop the rose quartz into the jar, and say, *"Rose quartz for love, respect, and friendship, one for you, and one for me."* Finally, add the turquoise, saying, *"Turquoise for harmony, happiness, and balance, one for you, and one for me."*

2. Pour the honey into the jar, and speak the words, *"Keep it sweet, keep it pure, keep it untainted. Our love is based on trust, loyalty, and respect. Never shall either of us stray."* Put the lid on the jar and bury it in your yard if you share a home, or place it under your bed if you and your lover live separately.

New Romance Oil

They say that scent can be an aphrodisiac. If you want to draw new romance into your life, blend a batch of this oil and wear a bit of it on your wrists and behind your ears to attract new love. Gather:

A pink candle
4 ounces base oil, such as grapeseed, jojoba, or sunflower
2 fresh apple blossoms, crushed
1 fresh chamomile flower, crushed
1 fresh yarrow flower, crushed
3 drops lavender essential oil
2 drops patchouli essential oil

Find a quiet place to work, and begin by lighting the candle. Pour your base oil into a bowl, and slowly add the herbs and oils. Swirl the bowl slowly in a clockwise direction to blend your ingredients, speaking the words, *"I have love to share and love to give. I call new love into my life. Draw new romance here to me, as I will, so it shall be."* Use your New Romance Oil to lightly anoint your skin—but don't overdo it—before you go out. Store your oil in a dark-colored bottle, and replenish as needed.

Crystal Charm to Improve Finances

At some point, we've all made financial decisions that felt like mistakes. Unfortunately, those mistakes can add up, leaving us caught in a vicious cycle of poor financial management and bad habits. If you find yourself stuck in this rut, craft a crystal charm to carry with you as a reminder to make better financial choices. Gather:

A penny, a nickel, and a dime
A small drawstring bag
1 piece of moss agate
1 piece of tiger's eye
1 piece of yellow topaz

1. Place the coins in the bag, and say, *"From this day on, my decisions are wise. They are thoughtful, they are responsible, and they will no longer do me harm."* Add the crystals, and say, *"I call money my way and will do as I must to make smart financial choices. I will be accountable for my decisions and will manifest abundance."*

2. Carry the drawstring bag in your pocket or purse. When you are facing a financial decision that could have a significant impact, take the bag out, hold it in your hands, and meditate on it while you consider the consequences of impulsive or foolish choices. Then, go make a smart decision.

Lodestone Money Attraction Spell

Lodestone is a natural magnet, so it's a perfect way to draw money into your life. By "feeding" your lodestone small bits of metal shavings, which are typically sold with the stone, you can attract money and abundance. Some people believe that money brought in by a lodestone should always be used to make more money, get into an investment, or build a business. Gather:

1 piece of lodestone
1 teaspoon of metal iron shavings
3 drops Money Oil (page 126)

Dab the Money Oil on your lodestone—you don't need much. Place the loadstone in a bowl in a location in your home where you will see it each day. Feed the stone with the metal shavings, and speak the words, *"Money, money, come to me, bless me with prosperity, growing more, every day, money, money, come my way."* Feed the stone and repeat the incantation every day when you walk past it. As money begins to come into your life, place some of it under the stone, to help attract even more.

Money Cookies

Chocolate is well known as an aphrodisiac, but a lot of people don't realize it's also associated with money magic, as are cashews and maple syrup. Combine them with a few other goodies to make these no-bake cookies, and you've got a winning bit of kitchen magic. Serve them to friends, or give them as gifts to help share the abundance. This recipe makes about 15 cookies. Gather:

¼ cup coconut oil
¼ cup pure maple syrup
½ cup unsweetened cocoa powder
⅓ cup cashew butter
1 cup rolled oats
⅓ cup brown sugar
1 teaspoon pure vanilla extract
½ teaspoon sea salt

1. In a pot over low heat, warm the coconut oil and maple syrup. Once they've melted enough to mix together, add the cocoa powder. Whisk in the cashew butter, and when it's fully blended in, remove the pot from the stove top.

2. Fold in the oats, brown sugar, vanilla, and sea salt. Stir the mixture in a clockwise direction, visualizing prosperity and financial abundance. Use a teaspoon to drop spoonfuls of the mixture onto a cookie sheet lined with parchment paper. (For easier use, spray the teaspoon with nonstick cooking spray.)

3. Refrigerate until the cookies are firm, and then enjoy them. Each time you take a bite, imagine the freedom that comes with prosperity.

Money Oil

Money Oil is a practical and useful magical item to have on hand. Blend a batch and incorporate it into workings as needed. Gather:

A gold or green candle
2 ounces base oil, such as grapeseed, jojoba, or sunflower
1 fresh basil leaf, crushed
½ teaspoon dried comfrey
3 drops cinnamon essential oil
2 drops sesame oil

1. Find a quiet place to work, and begin by lighting the candle. Pour your base oil into a bowl, and slowly add the herbs and oils. Swirl the bowl slowly in a clockwise direction to blend your ingredients, speaking the words, *"I call up only what I need, out of necessity, not out of greed. Money come and money grow, money in my wallet show."*

2. Place a couple of drops of Money Oil in your wallet or purse to draw money toward you. If you run a business, put a bit on or under the cash register to attract paying customers. If you're down to your last few dollars, dab some oil on the bills to make them multiply. Store your oil in a dark-colored bottle, and replenish as needed.

Prosperity Herbal Bath Sachet

When you're experiencing financial frustrations, a nice warm bath can help relieve your stress. Use this herbal bath sachet to give a little magical mojo to your bathwater and attract prosperity into your life. Gather:

A cloth drawstring bag, preferably green or gold

3 cinnamon sticks, broken into pieces

3 tablespoons dried chamomile flowers

3 tablespoons dried goldenrod

3 tablespoons dried patchouli

In a small dish, combine the herbs, then add them to the drawstring bag. Hang it over the faucet as you run a warm bath so that the water runs over the bag. As you soak in the tub, close your eyes and inhale the scent of the herbs. Visualize abundance and prosperity coming your way. Think about what changes you need to make; start planning to do things differently, and set yourself on the path to financial freedom.

Roadmap to Success Spell

Have you ever played a board game that involved collecting money? Sometimes, you end up back at your starting point with no money left in your hands at all—and other times, you're prosperous and successful. The game is a journey, just like real life, with steps forward and backward. This spell is similar to a board game, only you get to plan where you want to end up. Gather:

A piece of poster board
A green marker or felt-tip pen
1 piece of bloodstone

1. On the left edge of the poster board, use the green marker to write down your current financial situation, such as "getting by," or "living paycheck to paycheck," or "flat broke." On the right edge, write down your financial goal. Do you want to pay off a debt? Buy a new car? Save for your kids' college educations?

2. Between the two phrases, list all the things you'll need to do to reach your goal. It might include things like "get a second job" or "improve my credit score." With the marker, trace a path from your current situation, through your obstacles, to your ultimate goal. Draw as many lines as you need to connect all these different items together on your way to your goal.

3. Place your roadmap someplace where you can see it, and keep the bloodstone in your pocket. Each time you accomplish one of the tasks you listed, hold the bloodstone to that item on the board, and speak the words, *"One step closer, one step further, one more step down the road to success."* Cross items off as you finish them, and you'll find that soon you'll be at the end of your journey.

Calming Dream Pillow Sachet

Some herbs are associated with calm, dreams, and restful sleep. By incorporating them into a sachet to tuck into your pillow, you can bring about tranquil dreams, eliminate nightmares, and reduce agitation at bedtime. Use fresh herbs for this spell if at all possible. Gather:

<u>3 lavender stalks, fresh or dried</u>
<u>3 lilac flowers, fresh or dried</u>
<u>3 rosemary sprigs, fresh or dried</u>
<u>A drawstring bag</u>

Crush the herbs slightly between your fingertips to release their essential oils and fragrances. Take the time to inhale their scents and feel their calming vibrations. Speak the words, *"Good health, sweet dreams, rejuvenating sleep. A restful night lies ahead for me."* Fill the sachet with the herbs, bending them to fit if necessary, and place the sachet in your pillowcase at bedtime. Drift off to sleep with the aroma of magic surrounding you.

Crystal Water Sickroom Wash Spell

If you've got a friend or loved one who is chronically ill, this wash for the sickroom can help provide a bit of relief. You can sprinkle it around the room or on the bed; use it as a wash for doors, windows, and sheets; or even—with the doctor's permission—use it as a cleansing wash for the skin. Do this spell on the night of the full moon. Gather:

A clear jar with a lid
1 quart water
1 piece of carnelian
1 piece of moonstone
1 piece of selenite

Sit outside under the moonlight, pour the water into the jar, and then add the crystals. Hold the jar up to the moonlight so you can see it reflected in the water. Speak the words, *"By the magic of the moon, I call for healing for [Name]. I call for [Name] to be well, to be comforted, and to be blessed with healing energy. I send this healing magic with light and love."* Leave the jar outside overnight, and in the morning, remove the stones, cover the jar with the lid, and use the water as needed.

Crystal Wellness Talisman Spell

Crystals have a number of different therapeutic applications, and which ones you choose to work with will vary depending on the nature of the disorder. However, you can create this simple talisman for overall wellness and carry it with you as a preventive measure. Gather:

A blue candle
1 piece of agate
1 piece of amethyst
1 piece of jasper
A small blue drawstring pouch

1. Light the candle, and sit quietly, holding the three stones in your hands. Close your eyes, and feel the stones' vibrations as they work in harmony together. Feel their healing energies traveling through your hands, up your arms, and to the rest of your body.

2. Visualize this healing magic enveloping you like a warm cocoon, protecting you from illness, accidents, anxiety, and other maladies. Calmly speak the words, *"I am happy, I am healthy, I am hearty. I am whole, I am well, I am wonderful,"* as many times as you need to, while you feel the energies of the crystals.

3. When you feel their healing energy throughout your entire body, place the crystals in the bag, and carry it in your pocket or wear it on a cord around your neck to bring about general good health.

Healing Jar to Soothe Anxiety

If you're constantly feeling uneasy or nervous, a bit of healing magic can help in tandem with medical assistance. Do this working to help calm and soothe yourself when you are anxious. Gather:

A white candle

A small clear jar with a lid

3 dried sage leaves

1 piece of amethyst

1 piece of jet

1 tablespoon sea salt

9 drops Healing Oil (page 133)

Light the candle, and add the ingredients, one at a time, to the jar. As you add each one, speak the words, *"I am calm, I am cool, I am focused, I am attuned, I am healthy, and I am serene."* When you've added all the items to the jar, hold it between your hands, and take a moment to meditate. Think about how much happier you will be when you are calm and relaxed. Place the lid on the jar, and put the jar someplace where you can reach out and hold it whenever you're feeling anxious. Let the candle burn out on its own.

Healing Oil

The ancients used magical oils in rituals to heal the sick, and there's no reason you can't do the same thing. Blend a batch of healing oil to use in different ways; dress a candle for healing magic, anoint the bed of an ill person, or even dab it on your wrists to promote overall good health. If possible, do this spell outdoors on a sunny morning. Gather:

A blue candle
4 ounces base oil, such as grapeseed, jojoba, or sunflower
1 apple blossom, crushed
1 chamomile flower, crushed
1 dandelion flower, crushed
4 drops lavender essential oil
2 drops eucalyptus essential oil

1. Find a quiet place to work, and begin by lighting the candle. Pour your base oil into a bowl, and slowly add the herbs and oils. Swirl the bowl slowly in a clockwise direction to blend your ingredients, saying the words, *"I call health and wellness, well-being and calm. Illness and injury soon shall be gone."*

2. Use the oil as an aid to healing when someone is unwell or hurt, after they have consulted a physician or other medical professional. Store your oil in a dark-colored bottle, and replenish as needed.

Banishing Oil

Chances are you're not going to have to do a banishing spell on a regular basis, and that's definitely a good thing. However, it never hurts to be prepared. Blend this oil during the waning moon phase, and store it for later use so that you've got it on hand when it's really needed. Gather:

4 ounces base oil, such as grapeseed, jojoba, or sunflower
½ teaspoon black pepper
½ teaspoon cayenne pepper
½ teaspoon tobacco leaf, dried
½ teaspoon valerian, dried
1 teaspoon vinegar

1. Pour your base oil into a bowl, and slowly add the herbs, followed by the vinegar. Swirl the bowl slowly in a counterclockwise direction to blend your ingredients, speaking the words, *"Banishing negativity, I send it far away from me. All that is bad and all that is wrong, sent out of my life, forever gone."*

2. When you need to do a banishing, use a pin or other sharp object to write the name of the person or thing you wish to be rid of on a black candle, and then use your fingers to coat the candle in the Banishing Oil. Light the candle, and repeat the incantation. Allow the candle to burn out on its own. Store your oil in a dark-colored bottle.

Elemental Banishing Spell

A great method of banishing is the use of the four elements, Fire, Water, Earth, and Air. Water is used in a number of religions for banishing, and Fire is, quite obviously, a destructive force. Salt is representative of Earth and is often used to get rid of negative energy. Air can carry your problems away on the breeze. Try to time this working for the waning moon phase, and go someplace where you have access to a moving body of water, such as a river or creek. Gather:

A small garden trowel
4 small pieces of paper
½ cup sea salt
Matches
A fireproof bowl

Write the name of the person or thing you wish to banish on each of the four pieces of paper. Use the trowel to dig a small hole in the ground, and place one of the papers in the hole. Cover it with sea salt, and then bury it with the soil, reciting the words, *"I banish you by the power of Earth."* Take a second piece of paper, tear it into tiny pieces, and throw it into the wind, saying, *"I banish you by the power of Air."* Place the third paper in the fireproof bowl, light it with your matches, and say, *"I banish you by the power of Fire."* Finally, take the last piece of paper, tear it up, and throw it into the water. Now say, *"I banish you by the power of Water."* Take a moment to thank the four elements for aiding you with your problem, and think about it no more.

Simple Incense Cleansing Spell

If you need to do a basic cleansing of your home or other location, you can certainly do an elaborate ritual. However, you can create sacred space fairly easily with this simple spell. Use herbs associated with cleansing to create a loose incense blend. Gather:

1 teaspoon frankincense resin
1 teaspoon dried pine needles
1 teaspoon dried sweetgrass
1 teaspoon dried thyme
1 charcoal incense disc

1. In a small bowl, combine the resin, pine, sweetgrass, and thyme. Light the charcoal disc by carefully holding a match to it; the disc will spark when first lit, so be sure to place it in a fireproof bowl or brazier. Add 1 teaspoon of the loose incense blend; store the rest for later use.

2. As your incense begins to smoke, walk around your home, office, or other room, saying, *"Cleansing, purifying, smoke to the sky. Negative energy, gone by and by. Cleansing, purifying, blessing this place, I hereby declare this to be sacred space."* Repeat this spell as needed when you feel like the energy in your space needs a cleansing.

Binding Magic Spell Tablet

In ancient Greece and Rome, magical work was often done via the use of spell tablets. A spell tablet was a sheet of thinly rolled clay inscribed with the words of the spell. It was often used to keep one's enemies at bay, but it could also be incorporated into magic to prevent theft, assault, or deception. Gather:

2 small packages of modeling clay
A nail
12 inches of black ribbon

Knead the clay into a pliable ball. On a hard surface, flatten out the clay as thin as you can get it. Use the nail to inscribe into the surface of the clay the person's name and what you want them to stop doing, such as, *"I bind you, [Name], from causing harm to my friend [Name]."* Roll the clay into a tube, and tie it with the black ribbon. Go near the property of the person you're binding, without trespassing or otherwise breaking the law, and bury the spell tablet as close to their home as you can.

Blessing Oil

Blessing magic is a fairly generalized term, but you can create Blessing Oil to use with crystals, herbs, and other magical applications. Use it to anoint items such as candles for more specific types of magic. Gather:

2 ounces base oil, such as grapeseed, jojoba, or sunflower

3 drops patchouli essential oil

3 drops rosemary essential oil

5 drops sandalwood essential oil

Pour your base oil into a bowl, and slowly add the essential oils. Swirl the bowl slowly in a clockwise direction to blend your ingredients, speaking the words, *"I am blessed, I have good fortune, I have abundance, I have love."* Store your oil in a dark-colored bottle, and use as needed.

Good-Luck Candle Spell

In general, there's no all-purpose Good-Luck Candle Spell, because in magic, intent matters. What this means is that the color of the candle you use will be based on what sort of luck you want to see manifested. For instance, if you want to be lucky in love, use a pink candle. If you're hoping for good fortune in your career, try a gold or orange candle. A yellow candle can bring about luck in finding overall happiness. Try to do this spell during the waxing moon phase, for seven days. Gather:

A tall pillar candle in the appropriate color
A sharp knife
3 drops Blessing Oil (page 138)

Use the knife to create notches in the candle, dividing it into seven sections. Anoint the candle with the Blessing Oil. Light it, and concentrate on the flame. Visualize your intent, and draw that magical energy to you. Speak the words, *"Good luck in [intent] is coming to me. I call good fortune my way. From now on, I am lucky in [intent]."* Allow the candle to burn to the first notch, and then extinguish it. Repeat this each day so the spell begins to manifest over the course of seven days. You'll start to see your luck changing for the better.

Good-Luck Crystal Charm Spell

As with candle magic, there isn't a single good-luck spell involving crystals. Still, you can craft your own crystal charm depending on what kind of luck you hope to attain. For luck in protection, use agate or hematite. If you need luck in your marriage, work with rose quartz or emerald. Determine your purpose, and choose a crystal accordingly. Do this spell on a sunny day, if possible, early in the morning. Gather:

1 piece of crystal for the appropriate intent
30 inches of ribbon or cord in a corresponding color

Slowly wrap the crystal in the cord, chanting the words, *"With the power and energy of the sun, I call good luck to me. With the power and energy of the sun, I call good fortune to me. As this crystal is wrapped in this cord, I am wrapped in the light of the sun, and its rays will brighten my day."* Tie a knot in the cord and wear it around your neck as a good-luck talisman.

CHAPTER SIX
Meditations

Meditation can help calm the soul, celebrate various life milestones, and aid in offering gratitude to the universe. It also has healing benefits, promoting stress relief and mindfulness. This chapter contains 10 simple meditations for different times of day and for multiple celebrations of the human spirit. Try them all to see which ones resonate with you the most, and adjust them as needed to bring about change and magic in your day-to-day life.

"Meditation is a way for nourishing and blossoming the divinity within you."

—Amit Ray, *Meditation: Insights and Inspirations*

God and Goddess Healing Meditation

While healing magic is something you can share with others, you can absolutely work it on yourself! Regardless of how you choose to approach it, a healing meditation is a good way to heal an anxious or unwell body or soul. Do keep in mind that magic and meditation should be used in tandem with professional medical treatment and not as a substitute. Use this meditation to call upon the God and Goddess for assistance when you or a loved one feel off-kilter or ill. You can perform this meditation anytime or anyplace that it is needed.

1. Light a blue candle, and sit comfortably. If you have healing crystals on hand, such as amber, bloodstone, or clear quartz, place them on the parts of the body that are affected by illness or injury. Place statues of your goddesses and gods nearby if you've got them; this is a good way to connect to the Divine with prayer.

2. Speak the words, *"Goddess and God, Lady and Lord, I ask for your healing blessings. You are everywhere, in the universe and within my spirit, and you are light and love. I call upon you to bless me with health and wellness, and ask for this with gratitude and reverence. Goddess and God, Lady and Lord, I offer you my devotion, and release my intention to you and the universe. I thank you for your healing power, for your blessings, for your gifts, and for the love and light that flows within us all."*

3. Allow the candle to go out on its own, and place the crystals in your pocket or in a bag to keep with you or place in a sickroom. Go about your day knowing that the healing magic of the Divine is with you.

Gratitude Meditation

Many Wiccans believe in the law of attraction, which essentially means that by maintaining an attitude of gratitude and showing thankfulness, you can attract more positive things into your life. Perform this meditation anytime you wish to celebrate gratitude for your blessings. You may wish to have items that represent the things you are thankful for placed in front of you; these can be the actual items, photographs, or symbols.

1. Sit quietly, and consider all the things for which you are grateful. It can be anything that makes you feel fortunate and blessed—your family, your career, your health, and so on.

2. Enumerate your blessings out loud, like so: *"I am thankful that I am healthy. I am thankful for my family. I am thankful I get paid to do what I love. I am thankful for my friends who love and support me. I am thankful for my connection to the Divine."*

3. You may also wish to consider that there are people in your life who are grateful to you for the things *you* have done. After all, gratitude is a gift that keeps on giving, and counting our blessings is important, because it reminds us of how truly fortunate we are.

Meditation to Mourn and Remember

If you've lost someone you care about, it can be hard to move on. Use this meditation to honor a loved one who has passed away or otherwise transitioned out of your life. This meditation invokes the four elements as a way of honoring those who have died or been lost. Use symbols of Earth, Air, Fire, and Water for this meditation. A bowl of clean soil, a feather or incense, a small candle, and a cup of water will work. You'll also need some rosemary—fresh is best—which is associated with remembrance. If you have a photograph of the person or heirloom from the person you are honoring, include that as well.

1. Find a place to sit comfortably, and place the elemental symbols around you in the corresponding directions: Earth in the north, Air in the east, Fire in the south, and Water in the west.

2. Hold the rosemary in your hands, and inhale its fresh aroma. Speak the words, *"By the power of Earth from which we spring and then to which we return, I honor and remember you. By the power of Air, from which wisdom and intuition flow, I honor and remember you. By the power of Fire, which creates and yet destroys, I honor and remember you. By the power of Water, flowing off to the west, carrying you on your final journey, I honor and remember you."*

3. Call the person by name. Cry if you need to. Say, *"You were loved in life and shall be loved in death. As long as you are in my memory, a part of you lives on. I will not forget you, and will honor you with my words and deeds. You are loved, and you are remembered."*

4. When you're ready, end your meditation. Carry the rosemary with you, in your pocket or in a sachet, as a reminder of your lost loved one.

Meditation to Celebrate Love

They say love is a many-splendored thing. When you're fortunate enough to have it in your life, it's sacred and worth celebrating. Use this meditation to rejoice in the love you have, whether it's love with a romantic partner, love of your family, the love of the Divine, or even self-love.

1. Begin by lighting a pink candle and holding a piece of rose quartz in your hands. Focus on the crystal, and feel its vibrations spreading from your hands up through your arms, into your chest, and reaching your heart.

2. Concentrate on the stone, and speak the words, *"Love is in my life, love is in my heart, love is in my world. I am blessed, I am complete, I am happy. Love has come to me, and for that I am grateful. I accept love unconditionally, and I return it freely, because love is a sacred gift."*

3. Feel the love radiating outward from your heart and surrounding you with a warm, soft, pink glow. Say, *"My heart is full, my world is full, my life is full of love. I celebrate love, in all of its forms, pure and light and joyful."* Others will be able to sense that your heart is a welcoming one, and they'll respond accordingly.

Meditation to Start Your Day

A meditation to kick off your morning can set the tone for your entire day. You can perform this meditation just as the sun comes up to begin your day on a positive note. Do this outdoors if you can, or in front of an east-oriented window so you can feel the sun's glow upon your face.

1. Begin by lighting a gold or yellow candle and incense with a fragrance associated with the sun, such as frankincense.

2. Sit comfortably with your hands in your lap, close your eyes, and speak the words, *"The night has passed, and the wheel has turned once more. Darkness is leaving. The sun rises again, and with it comes light and hope. It illuminates my path, brightens my way, and guides me throughout the day."*

3. As you sit, steady your breathing so you are inhaling and exhaling calmly and slowly. Open your eyes, and watch as the sun begins its ascent above the horizon. Listen to the changes in the air around you. Do you hear different sounds as the world awakens? Is there a sense of something alive that wasn't there before?

4. Once the sun has completely broken, raise your hands out to welcome it. Say, *"Light has come, day has broken, and the earth arises from its slumber. Today is a new day, full of new beginnings. I am full of light and hope, like the sun, and I am grateful to have this fresh day. I am blessed to be alive, and thankful for the gift."*

5. Extinguish the candle, let the incense burn out on its own, and begin your day rejuvenated and revitalized.

Meditation to End Your Day

In today's world, it's easy to get stressed out and emotionally drained by the time evening rolls around. After all, you had a long, busy day filled with challenges! Get your spirit and soul settled down with this meditation as the day comes to an end. Perform this meditation after dark, at bedtime, when you can be alone and undisturbed.

1. Begin by turning out the lights and lighting a blue candle; blue is associated with calming energy. As you sit in the near darkness, take a moment to reflect upon your day. What are some positive things that happened? Was there anything you said or did that made you especially proud or happy? Watch the candle as the flame dances in the darkness.

2. Speak the words, "The day has ended, the sun has set, darkness has fallen. I have accomplished much today, and there is still more for me to achieve tomorrow. I am blessed to be alive, and as I sleep tonight, I will journey peacefully through the world of dreams. I am healthy and whole, and I welcome the quiet of the night."

3. Close your eyes and breathe deeply, inhaling and exhaling, feeling your body becoming attuned to the rhythms of the darkness. Clear your mind of all the things that have caused you stress throughout the day, and know you can handle them when you're fresh in the morning. Say, "The night is here and I embrace it as I fall into peaceful slumber. I will awaken refreshed and clear, ready to take on any challenges I may face." Extinguish the candle and go to bed.

Thanking the Gods and Goddesses

Sometimes, we meditate or pray simply to show the deities that we respect and value them. We don't always have to ask for something from them; in fact, just showing appreciation for them can go a long way. After all, our relationship with the goddesses and gods shouldn't be transactional. Show them how much you value them, and they'll more than likely respond in kind, without your even asking.

1. Light a pair of white candles to represent the Goddess and God. If you'd like to make an offering, do so; this can be food, wine, items you've crafted by hand, or even a song, poem, or painting.

2. Speak, *"Goddess and God, Lady and Lord, I honor you today. Thank you for standing by my side, and for walking with me when I needed you. Thank you for blessing me with the chance to give and receive unconditional love. Thank you for all your gifts, your bounty, and your abundance. Thank you, Lady and Lord, for showing me how to love myself and for helping my spirit soar. Thank you for giving me the opportunity to share myself with others, and for watching over me each day. God and Goddess, Lord and Lady, I honor you today."*

3. Meditate quietly, feeling the presence of the Divine around you. When you are finished, extinguish the candles.

Mindfulness Meditation

Mindfulness is the practice of being deliberately cognizant of things both around and inside you. By achieving conscious mindfulness, we become actively aware of the present. On a spiritual level, this clarity can help us attune ourselves to the connection between the Divine and ourselves. Try to do this meditation outside, at any time of day.

1. Begin by lighting a white candle, and hold a piece of selenite. You may wish to burn incense in a fragrance associated with spiritual development, such as myrrh or sandalwood. Close your eyes, and focus all your attention on the center of your body. Breathe calmly, in and out.

2. Speak or chant, *"I am aware, I am awake, I am connected to the Divine."*

3. As you breathe, consider the sensory stimuli around you. Do you smell freshly cut grass or wood smoke? Can you hear leaves rustling or birds singing? Perhaps there's a cool breeze blowing over your skin, or warm sunlight on your face. Pay attention, and attune your body to the natural world.

4. Say, *"Deliberate clarity is mine to embrace. I am aware, I am awake, I am conscious of all things, and I am connected to the Divine."*

5. Continue calm breathing, and when you are ready, end your meditation by extinguishing the candle. Carry the piece of selenite, charged by this mindful energy, with you as a reminder of your awareness.

Success Meditation

Who doesn't want to be successful? The first step is to define what success means to you. Is it about financial freedom? Perhaps you'd like to achieve a lifelong dream or goal, like finally getting your degree, starting your own business, or learning how to skydive. Use this simple meditation to bring about success, whether it's in your professional life or your personal one. Try to do this during the waxing moon phase to attract success and abundance to you.

1. Light a gold or green candle. If you have a crystal or stone associated with success, such as an emerald or diamond, hold it in your hands. Close your eyes, and envision the goals you've set for yourself. Be as specific as possible. Now consider what steps you'll need to take to achieve your ambitions.

2. Speak the words, *"I call success my way, I call abundance my way, I call purpose my way, I call vision my way. I will work hard, overcoming obstacles, and never wavering in my intent. I will pursue my dreams, sharing my talents and skills for the greater good. I will strive to be my best, to do my best, and will reap the benefits of my own efforts. I call success my way, I call abundance my way, I call purpose my way, I call vision my way."*

3. Extinguish the candle, carry or wear the stone you've charged with your successful intent, and go be the best person you possibly can; remember, success will be your reward!

White Light Calming Meditation

It's been shown that people who meditate typically experience less stress, and if you can incorporate meditation into your daily routine, you'll benefit mentally, spiritually, and physically. This calming meditation is one you can do anywhere, anytime you're feeling stressed out. While you can certainly include a candle or incense as part of this exercise if you like, it's specifically designed so that you can do it with no materials or accessories at all.

1. Close your eyes and imagine yourself surrounded by a soft white light. As you do so, concentrate on your breath as you inhale and exhale. If you are consciously thinking about your breathing, you're not focusing on all the things that have been worrying or upsetting you.

2. As you calm your breath, speak the words, *"The past is gone, and there are things beyond my control. I will not worry about them, and I will not dwell upon the past. Instead, I will focus on moving forward."*

3. Keep your eyes closed, and visualize that white light moving in and out of your body, with your breath, spreading throughout your insides. As it moves through your chest, down into your diaphragm, through your arms and legs, picture the calm healing energy traveling through every cell of your being.

4. Say, *"I am calm and comfortable, and I am at peace. I am in control, I have power, and things that frustrate me will not defeat me. I am whole in body, mind, and spirit."* Continue to breathe in and out, and when you are completely relaxed, end your meditation and go about your day.

5. Feel the love radiating outward from your heart and surrounding you with a warm, soft, pink glow. Say, *"My heart is full, my world is full, my life is full of love. I celebrate love in all of its forms, pure and light and joyful."*

6. Others will be able to sense that your heart is a welcoming one, and they'll respond accordingly.

CHAPTER SEVEN
Rituals

itual is the foundation of much of Wiccan practice. Ritual, in general, should be celebratory. Whether it's to mark a Sabbat holiday, a phase of the moon, the changing of the seasons, or a milestone in your life, ritual is a way of bringing yourself closer to the Divine and developing spiritually. You can write a ritual of your own to celebrate just about anything, but to get you started, here are 10 rituals that focus on common purposes and will give you a solid foundation for more complex ritual work later. You can use more than one of them at a time; for instance, you can begin with Casting a Circle (see page 157), move on to the Healing Ritual (see page 159), and then close with the Cakes and Ale Ceremony (see page 155).

One important note on Wiccan ritual: Some people start their rituals facing north, and others facing east, depending on which tradition of Wicca they have studied. Although the following are written with the directions beginning in the north, you can certainly rearrange them to begin in the east if you choose to.

"On every full moon, rituals . . . take place on hilltops, beaches, in open fields, and in ordinary houses. Writers, teachers, nurses, computer programmers, artists, lawyers, poets, plumbers, and auto mechanics—women and men from many backgrounds come together to celebrate the mysteries of the Triple Goddess of the Dance of Life."

—Starhawk, *The Spiral Dance: A Rebirth of the Ancient Religion of the Goddess*

152

Ancestor Ritual

For many Wiccans and other members of the Pagan community, emphasis is placed on honoring one's ancestors. Although you may want to do an ancestor ritual specifically at Samhain—a time of ancestor veneration—you can do one at any point during the year. It's a great way to honor long-departed family members and ask those of your bloodline to watch over you.

1. Instead of using your regular altar, decorate your dinner table with family photos and heirlooms. If you have ashes from a family member or a photo of his or her gravestone, even better! Have you traced your family tree? Add a genealogy chart! If a relative has passed away recently, place a white candle for them on the table. You can light additional candles for other loved ones, and as you do so, say the person's name aloud. Use tea lights for this, especially if you have a lot of relatives to honor.

2. Have a meal prepared to eat as part of your ritual. If possible, include dark bread, autumn vegetables, apples, and even cider or wine; all these are foods associated with the ancestors and the world of the dead. Set your table with a place for you and a place for the ancestors. Finally, light some rosemary incense, which is associated with remembrance.

3. There is no need to cast the circle before you begin this ritual. After you have lit all the candles for your ancestors, speak the words, *"Tonight is a night in which I call out to those who came before me. Tonight I honor my ancestors. I call to you, and welcome you to join me for this night. You watch over me always, protecting and guiding me, and tonight I thank you. Please, blood of my blood, join me and share in my meal."*

4. Serve yourself a helping of whatever foods you have prepared, except for the wine or cider, and place a serving on the ancestors' plate. As you eat, take the time to recall stories of kinfolk who are no longer among the living. This is the time to remember the summers you spent with your grandma in the mountains or your uncle's war stories or the story about that time when your great-grandfather won a cow in a drunken poker game.

(continued)

5. When you are finished eating, pour the cider or wine in a cup for yourself and one for your ancestors. Take a sip, and speak your genealogy aloud, like so: *"I am Willow, daughter of Mary, who was the daughter of Eugene, the son of . . ."* and so forth. You don't have to go back to the beginning of time, but try to include at least a couple of generations that are deceased. You can even add in qualifiers, such as *"Daughter of Bill, who fought in Vietnam, the son of Margaret, who came here from the old country . . ."*

6. After you have recited your ancestry to the best of your ability, raise your cup in a toast to your departed family members, and say, *"This is the cup of remembrance. I remember all of you in my heart. Kith and kin, clan and family, blood of my blood, you are dead but never forgotten, and you live on within me."* Drink from your cup, and consider what you will do to make your ancestors proud of you.

A quick note here: If you are adopted, you are fortunate enough to be able to choose whether you wish to honor your adoptive ancestors or your biological ones. You can even pay tribute to a combination of the two. If you don't know your birth family's ancestry, it's perfectly okay to say, *"Daughter of a family unknown"* in this ritual. Do what makes you the most comfortable.

Cakes and Ale Ceremony

In many Wiccan traditions, a ritual session is completed with a ceremony called Cakes and Ale. This is more than just post-ritual snack time; it's a way of formally ending the time spent in the sacred circle and thanking the God and Goddess for their blessing. The "cakes" are not typically cakes at all but cookies, often baked in the shape of a crescent moon. While the "ale" can be alcoholic, many Wiccans opt to use cider, juice, or even water instead.

You'll need a cake or cookies; you can certainly use something commercially purchased, but it's traditional for them to be homemade. To make your own cookies for this ceremony, use this simple recipe.

Crescent Ritual "Cakes"

¾ cup soft butter (real butter, not margarine)
1 cup granulated white sugar
1 cup brown sugar
2 eggs
1 tablespoon lemon juice

2 teaspoons lemon zest
2 cups flour or gluten-free baking mix
½ cup finely chopped almonds
Confectioners' sugar (optional)

1. In a large mixing bowl, cream the butter, and gradually stir in the sugar and brown sugar. Add the eggs, lemon juice, and zest, and mix well. Stir in the flour and the almonds until the dough is uniform.

2. Cover the bowl with plastic wrap and refrigerate overnight. When you are ready to make the "cakes," preheat the oven to 375°F and grease a cookie sheet.

3. Shape the firmly chilled dough into 12 to 15 crescent moon shapes by hand. Place them 3 inches apart on the cookie sheet. Bake for 8 to 10 minutes.

4. If you'd like, sprinkle them with confectioners' sugar when they come out of the oven and are still warm. You can serve these warm and fresh for ritual or store them for later use.

(continued)

The Ceremony

Your Crescent Ritual "Cakes" and ale (or other beverage you've chosen) should be on your altar or somewhere within your sacred circle before you begin. You'll also need your athame.

1. After you have concluded all your other magical work, pour yourself a cup of the beverage you've chosen. Hold it up before the altar, and speak the words, *"I give thanks to the Goddess for her blessings. She watches over me in this sacred space, and I am grateful to her."*

2. Raise your athame in your dominant hand, and hold it up, saying, *"I give thanks to the God for his blessings. He watches over me in this sacred space, and I am grateful to him."*

3. Lower the athame into the cup and say, *"I give thanks to the God and Goddess together for their blessings. As they join together, may they bring abundance and fruitfulness into my life. So mote it be."* Take a drink of the ale, and place the cup back on the altar.

4. Next, raise your ritual cake before the altar. Speak the words, *"May the God and Goddess bless this food and guide my daily life. They walk beside me always, nourishing and enriching my soul and spirit. I am privileged and honored to know them, and thankful for their magic and wisdom. So mote it be."* Eat your cake.

5. Take a moment to think about the blessings you have in your life, and consider how you may share that bounty with others as a way of honoring the gods.

Casting a Circle

In many Wiccan traditions, casting a circle is an integral part of any larger ritual. While you certainly don't have to do it every single time you perform a ritual, knowing how to do so will allow you to build on the framework of creating sacred space prior to magical workings. Remember, a circle is used not only to mark your space as sacred but also to keep good energy in, and negative energy away. When you begin other rituals, you may want to begin by casting a circle.

1. First, determine how large you want your sacred space to be—seven to nine feet in diameter should be plenty of room for one person—and mark it on the floor or ground with chalk, string, salt, or even birdseed. Put any magical tools you'll be using on the altar in the center, and place a candle in each of the four directions. Use brown or green in the north for Earth, yellow in the east for Air, orange or red in the south representing Fire, and blue in the west for Water. Hold your athame in your dominant hand.

2. Start by lighting the green or brown candle in the north, and with your athame raised up, speak the words, *"Guardians of the North, I call upon you to watch over my rituals. Powers of endurance and strength, guided by Earth, I ask you to keep me safe inside this circle. Let this space be sacred and blessed. So mote it be."*

3. Next, light the candle to the east, raise your athame up and say, *"Guardians of the East, I call upon you to watch over my rituals. Powers of knowledge and wisdom, guided by Air, I ask you to keep me safe inside this circle. Let this space be sacred and blessed. So mote it be."*

4. Light the candle in the south, and keep your athame out, arm extended pointing southward. Now say, *"Guardians of the South, I call upon you to watch over my rituals. Powers of energy and will, guided by Fire, I ask you to keep me safe inside this circle. Let this space be sacred and blessed. So mote it be."*

(continued)

5. Finally, light the candle in the west, raise your athame, and speak the words, *"Guardians of the West, I call upon you to watch over my rituals. Powers of emotion and passion, guided by Water, I ask you to keep me safe inside this circle. Let this space be sacred and blessed. So mote it be."*

6. Return to the center of your circle, raise the athame high in both hands, and say, *"The circle is now cast, and this is sacred space. So mote it be."* Begin doing any other magical workings you have planned.

Dismissing the Circle

When you've concluded your magical workings, you have a couple of options for dismissing the circle.

1. Some people walk back around the circle in a counterclockwise direction and extinguish the candles. If you do this, you can say farewell to the elements as you dismiss them, like this: *"Guardians of the North, I thank you for watching over my rituals. Powers of endurance and strength, guided by Earth, thank you for keeping me safe inside this circle. The circle is now dismissed. So mote it be."*

2. If you prefer to keep things simple, you can follow a method that some Wiccan groups use. Walk around the circle, beginning at the north and moving counterclockwise, athame raised outward. When you return to the northernmost part of the circle, kiss the blade of your athame (be conscious of sharp edges!) and say, *"This ritual has ended, and the circle is dismissed."*

Healing Ritual

Healing magic can be done for yourself or on behalf of others. If you opt to perform this ritual on behalf of someone else who is ill or injured, do keep in mind that many Wiccans believe you should ask that person for permission before doing any sort of magic. On the other hand, some people feel that if you have implied permission—that you genuinely think the other person would want you to do this on their behalf—you may go ahead and do it. The person does not have to be present for you to do this ritual. In some cases, if someone is terminally ill, they may not want healing done at all. Instead, they may be wishing for their pain to end. This is why it may be wise to ask permission before performing the ritual.

1. You'll need a blue candle with your friend's name inscribed on it and a loose incense blend of equal parts apple blossom, lemon balm, sandalwood, and yarrow; make sure you have a charcoal disc and a fireproof holder for your incense.

2. Begin by casting a circle to create sacred space. When you are ready to begin, raise your hands to the sky, and speak the words, *"Great Goddess and God, I call upon you to ask your assistance for one who is ill. [Name] is ailing, and needs your healing energy. Watch over [Name] and offer strength and wellness. Keep [Name] safe from further illness. Protect [Name]'s body and soul in this time of sickness."*

3. Light the charcoal disc and place your incense blend on it. As the smoke begins to rise, envision illness and disease traveling away with the smoke. Say, *"Great Goddess and God, I ask that you take away [Name]'s illness, carrying it off on the four winds, that it may never return."*

4. Turn to face the north, and say, *"To the north, I send this illness away, that it may be replaced with strength."*

5. Face east, saying, *"To the east, I send this illness away, that it may be replaced with health."*

(continued)

6. Turn to the south, and say, *"To the south, I send this illness away, that it may be replaced with vitality."*

7. Finally, face west, and speak the words, *"To the west, I send this illness away, that it may be replaced with life. Carry it away from [Name], and scatter it so that it will be no more."*

8. Close your eyes and envision your friend's illness as a dark cloud. Picture it leaving that person's body, gradually moving up to the sky and dissipating into the winds. Imagine it drifting away, breaking up into small and insignificant pieces so that your friend will be healthy, happy, and whole.

9. When you are ready to move on, say, *"Hail to you, great Goddess and God. I pay you tribute each day, and ask only this one small blessing. May your love and light surround [Name], supporting [him or her], healing [him or her], and strengthening [him or her] in this time of illness and pain."*

10. Light the candle. Say, *"[Name], I light this candle in your honor tonight. I have asked the gods to watch over you, keeping you in their loving embrace. I have asked that they guide and heal you, bringing you comfort and easing your pain. May they care for you in your time of illness and embrace you with their healing energy."*

11. Take a few moments to meditate on what you really wish for your friend, and to silently thank the gods once again for their assistance. When you are finished, leave the candle on your altar to burn out on its own.

> **"This is what rituals are for. We do spiritual ceremonies as human beings in order to create a safe resting place for our most complicated feelings of joy or trauma, so that we don't have to haul those feelings around with us forever, weighing us down. We all need such places of ritual safekeeping."**
>
> —Elizabeth Gilbert, *Eat, Pray, Love*

Monthly Esbat Ritual

In addition to celebrating the eight Sabbats during the year, most Wiccans also celebrate the full moon each month. A full moon ritual, or Esbat, is a celebration in which magic is performed and the gods are honored. The word *Esbat* comes from the French *s'esbattre*, which roughly means to "frolic joyfully." Commune with the gods, frolic joyfully while you're at it, and make some magic!

1. If possible, do this ritual outdoors. You'll need a bowl of water on your altar, along with a white candle and four pieces of moonstone. Begin by casting a circle and placing the moonstones around the white candle so they are oriented to the four directions. You may even wish to decorate your altar with lunar symbols such as moon statues, silver ribbons, or mirrors.

2. Turn to face your altar, arms open wide and palms up, and face the moon up in the sky. Speak the words, *"Bright Goddess, night queen, mistress of tides, keeper of women's intuition, I greet you! You are ever changing yet endless, ever moving yet stable. Guide me with your wisdom, allow me the awareness of intuition, and watch over me, keeping me in your soft embrace."*

3. Light the candle, and take a moment to meditate upon the blessings in your life. If you're doing this ritual each month, think about what has transpired since the last time you performed it.

4. Hold the bowl of water up to the moon, and say, *"Moon goddess, great mother, watch over me night and day. Bring with you the changing of the tides, the shifting of the shadows, the flow of women's bodies, the passion of lovers beneath your light. Your wisdom is great, your light is eternal, and I honor you. Keep your watchful eye upon me as you ebb and flow, wax and wane, and cycle once more to fullness. Moon goddess, great mother, I thank you for your blessings."*

(continued)

5. Place the bowl back on the altar so that the moonlight is reflected in the water, and raise your arms to the sky once more. Close your eyes, and speak the words, *"Moon goddess, great mother, you are universal and constant. In the dark of night, you bathe us in your light and love. I am grateful to feel your presence within my heart. You look down upon the desert sands, upon the roaring tide, upon the mighty forests, upon the endless plains, upon the vast mountains, and you look down upon me this night. Moon goddess, great mother, I honor you."*

6. Bask for a while in the glow of the moonlight. When you are ready to move forward with additional rituals or magical workings, do so. Carry the moonstones in your pockets or place them under your pillow at night, and use the moon water over the next month for watering plants, making offerings, or doing other spellwork.

Protection Ritual

One of the most practical and effective uses of magic is that of protection. Do this ritual to protect your hearth and home, and all the people who live with you.

1. You'll need a bowl of soil from your yard or nearby, a brown candle inscribed with your address to represent the land itself, and one piece of hematite for each door into your house. There is no need to cast a circle because you will be establishing your property as sacred space.

2. Begin at the part of your home that gets the most foot traffic; for most people, this will be the front door. Place the bowl of soil in front of the door. Put your hands in the soil and feel its secure earth energy traveling through your fingertips and spreading throughout the rest of your body.

3. Focus on it for a moment, and speak the words, *"Earth, soil, land, stable and strong, bring peace and harmony into my home. My family is well, my house is a haven, and my hearth is a place of blessings and hospitality for all who enter. Earth, soil, land, ground me and protect me and mine. This property is a safe and sacred space, full of harmony and love."*

4. Leave the bowl in front of your door, and begin walking the perimeter of your property, traveling clockwise. As you reach each door of your home, place a hematite stone on the ground in front of it. As you do, say, *"Protect my home, my family, my possessions, my spirit, all that which is mine. Keep out what would cause harm, allow no passage to those who would bring danger into our lives."* Repeat this process at every door.

5. When you return to your bowl of soil at the entrance, light your candle, and place it within the bowl. Pack the soil lightly around it so that the candle doesn't fall over. Speak the words, *"Fire and Earth, brought together, bringing balance and harmony, passion and security. This house is a home, this house is a haven, and none shall trespass here. So mote it be."*

6. Take a few moments to reflect on your home life, and the things that mean security to you. When you are finished, bring the bowl and the candle inside, and place it on your hearth or kitchen table. Allow the candle to burn out on its own. When it has, bury the candle near your front door.

Rituals to Ground and Center

Grounding and centering are, in many Wiccan traditions, an important component of ritual. Centering is a way of focusing your energy prior to beginning magical work, and the practice of grounding will allow you to eliminate excess energy you may have built up during spellwork or ritual. If you get into the habit of centering prior to magical work and grounding afterward, you'll be able to remain a lot more focused during rituals and function more effectively when you leave your sacred space.

Centering

Centering can be used to calm you and get you focused prior to any significant magical working. The best part about centering? You don't need any tools or supplies to make it work, and you can center anywhere! A great place to do it is inside your sacred space after you've cast a circle and before you begin magical work.

1. Stand at your altar, take a deep breath, and exhale slowly. Repeat this a few times, until your breath is even and regular. Some people find it easier to regulate their breathing if they count or chant a simple tone as they inhale and exhale, but you don't have to.

2. Once your breathing is regulated and even, begin visualizing magical energy. Touch the palms of your hands lightly together, rubbing gently as though you were trying to warm them, and then move them slightly apart. You should feel a tingling sensation, almost like an electrical charge, between your palms. That's magical energy! Don't panic if you don't feel it at first; just try it again, and after a few tries, you'll notice that the gap between your hands seems to have a bit of resistance.

3. Picture that tingly area expanding and contracting, in and out, and then visualize it enveloping your whole body.

4. Each time you center, repeat this process, and eventually it should come as second nature to you. You'll be able to center anytime or anyplace. By learning to do this, you'll develop a foundation for more advanced magical work as you develop your abilities.

Grounding

After you've concluded a ritual, you may find yourself hyperaware and even a bit jittery. That's not uncommon; after all, ritual raises energy. If you haven't centered properly beforehand, you can be a little bit off-kilter afterward; learning how to ground can alleviate that.

1. Much like centering, grounding involves the manipulation of energy; however, instead of drawing that energy inside you and then surrounding yourself with it, you'll push it out, away from yourself. Close your eyes and focus, regulating your breath. Imagine your energy as a light coursing through your body. Rein it back so that it becomes concentrated in one area, and gradually allow it to travel into your legs, down to your feet. Visualize that energy in your toes, and then picture it leaving your body, traveling down into the ground and dissipating away.

2. Some people prefer to send excess energy through their hands and fling it into the air, but if you're inexperienced, this should be done with caution; if you're around other magically minded folk, one of them could absorb what you're getting rid of, and then they're in exactly the same state you were just in.

3. Feel that excess power draining away, as if you had pulled a plug out of the bathtub. You may even find it helpful to bounce lightly on your toes for a moment to help shake out the last of that residual energy. Once you've finished and are calm, move on to whatever you plan to do next.

Ritual to Honor the Goddess and God

In many Wiccan traditions, the Goddess and God are honored together. They are spiritual peers, and there is a polarity to the Divine in which the feminine and masculine are equally sacred. Do this ritual to celebrate your relationship with them. If there is a specific god or goddess that you connect to, you can certainly call upon that diety by name during this rite.

1. You'll need a food offering, such as bread, on your altar for this ritual, as well as a cup of wine or milk and a pair of white candles. Inscribe the candles with symbols so that one represents the God and the other the Goddess, and light incense in a scent associated with the Divine, such as frankincense. Decorate your altar with representations of the God, like antlers, acorns, pinecones, and other phallic symbols. To symbolize the magic of the Goddess, use flowers (especially red ones), cups, seashells, and other feminine items.

2. Cast a circle before you begin this ritual. When you are ready, take a moment to close your eyes and welcome the Divine into your sacred space. Light the Goddess candle, and say, *"I light this candle in honor of the Goddess. She is the maiden, the mother, the crone. She is wisdom, intuition, and love."*

3. Light the God candle, speaking the words, *"I light this candle in honor of the God. He is the horned god, the mighty stag, the wise old sage. He is passion, energy, and fertility."*

4. Take the food offering and walk slowly around your circle in a clockwise direction. When you return to the altar, say, *"May the blessings of the Goddess be upon me. May I never hunger."*

5. Walk the circle again, this time with your wine or milk. When you reach the altar once more, say, *"May the blessings of the God be upon me. May I never hunger."*

6. Take a moment to think about the blessings and bounty the gods have brought into your life. For what do you owe them thanks? How can you show them your appreciation? What can you do to honor them in the future, by words or actions?

7. Say, *"These candles are lit for home and hearth, for fire and fertility, for the sacred masculine and the divine feminine. The mother and father, the Goddess and God, watch over me tonight as I pay them tribute. Hail to the great Goddess and her mighty consort, the powerful God! Great Goddess, fair maiden, fertile mother, wise crone. Mighty God, keeper of the forest, wild stag, wise sage. I honor you both this night. I thank you for all you provide, and ask your blessings. So mote it be."*

8. Again, take time to consider the gifts that the gods have given you, and consider ways to show them gratitude in the future.

Self-Dedication Ritual

In traditional Wiccan covens, new members are welcomed with an initiation ritual. If you're practicing alone, you can't self-initiate; by its very definition, initiation requires the participation of another person. However, what you *can* do is self-dedicate yourself to Wicca and to the gods you have chosen to honor. This is a way to formally declare your commitment to a new belief system, and to the Divine. Some people wait until they have spent a year and a day studying prior to performing a self-dedication ritual, but that is entirely up to you.

1. Try to time this ritual so it coincides with the new moon phase; this is, after all, a time of new beginnings. You'll need some Blessing Oil (see page 138), a white candle, and a tablespoon of sea salt. If you'd like to cast a circle, go ahead and do so. Then stand before your altar, and begin by centering, allowing yourself to become good and relaxed. Clear your mind of all the things in your mundane life that distract you and stress you out—forget about your job, your kid's messy room, and whether or not your spouse took out the trash. Focus on your inner peace and the tranquility to which you're entitled.

2. When you're ready to proceed, sprinkle the salt on the floor or ground, and stand upon it, barefoot. Light the candle, and watch the flame. Think about the goals you will set for yourself on your spiritual journey and your motivations for dedicating yourself to the gods. Raise your hands to the skies, and speak the words, *"I am a child of the Goddess and God, and ask them to bless me today."*

3. Dip a finger into the Blessing Oil, and with your eyes closed, anoint your forehead by lightly tracing a pentagram on your skin. Say, *"My mind is blessed that I may accept the wisdom of the Goddess and God."*

4. Next, lightly anoint your eyelids with a drop of the oil (eyes closed, and be careful not to get it in your eyes!), and say, *"My eyes are blessed, that I may see clearly upon my path."* Anoint the tip of your nose in the same manner. Say, *"My nose is blessed, that I may breathe in the essence of the Divine."*

5. Lightly anoint your lips, again using just a drop of oil, and say, *"My lips are blessed, that I may always speak truthfully and honorably."* Touch a bit more oil to your chest, saying, *"My heart is blessed, that I may give and receive love."*

6. Anoint the backs of your hands in the same way. Say, *"My hands are blessed, that I may heal and help others."* Next, anoint your genital area (again, be extra careful with the oil around sensitive skin) and speak the words, *"My womb (or if you identify as male, your phallus) is blessed, that I may create life."*

7. Next, anoint the soles of your feet with the oil, and say, *"My feet are blessed, that I may walk side by side and hand in hand with the Goddess and God."*

8. Focus once more on the candle flame burning before you, and feel the light of the gods moving through your body. Say, *"Tonight, I pledge myself to the Goddess and God, and to this new path upon which I walk. The gods are beside me, and I ask them to guide me on this journey. I will honor them with my words and actions. So mote it be."*

9. Take a few moments to meditate quietly. Listen to see if the gods are speaking to you. Feel their energy and light around you. Now that you have brought yourself to their attention, be sure to accept the gift of their wisdom and insight when it is offered.

Tool Consecration Ritual

As you acquire magical tools of your own—an athame, crystals, a wand, and others—it's a good idea to consecrate them prior to using them for the first time. This will purify the item before you use it to interact with the Divine, and it also removes any negative energy from the tool—especially if you aren't sure of its past history or who handled it before it came to you. This ritual is a simple one that can be used to dedicate your magical tools, clothing, jewelry, or even the altar itself. Use the four elements to consecrate your tools so they are blessed with pure intent. Cast a circle before you begin this ritual.

1. Place the items you wish to bless on your altar. In addition, light incense in a fragrance associated with cleansing and purification, such as frankincense or hyssop. Place this on the east side of your altar. On the south side of the altar, light a white candle. On the west side, place a bowl or chalice of moon-consecrated water. Finally, on the north side of your altar, place a bowl of salt.

2. Begin by passing the tool over the bowl of salt, and speak the words, *"Powers of the North, Guardians of Earth, I consecrate this tool and charge it with your magical energy. It is pure and sacred, and I will use it wisely."*

3. Pass the item through the incense smoke, saying, *"Powers of the East, Guardians of Air, I consecrate this tool and charge it with your magical energy. It is pure and sacred, and I will use it wisely."*

4. Next, move the item over the candle flame (taking care if it's a flammable item!), and say, *"Powers of the South, Guardians of Fire, I consecrate this tool and charge it with your magical energy. It is pure and sacred, and I will use it wisely."*

5. Finally, pass your tool over the chalice of water, speaking the words, *"Powers of the West, Guardians of Water, I consecrate this tool and charge it with your magical energy. It is pure and sacred, and I will use it wisely."*

6. Once you have consecrated the object with the help of the four elements, it is time to claim ownership of it. This establishes a magical connection between you and the wand, Book of Shadows, or whatever it may be. Hold the item up to the sky and call out, *"I charge this tool by the powers of Earth, of Air, of Fire, and of Water. I claim it as my own in the name of the Old Ones, the Ancients, the Goddess and God, the sun, the moon, and the stars. I banish any negativity, and make it new and fresh. I consecrate this tool, and claim it as mine!"*

7. Many Wiccans believe that once you've consecrated a tool, you should put it to use immediately; this binds the consecration and strengthens the energy of the tool. You can use some freshly consecrated tools, like an athame, chalice, or wand to consecrate other tools. If you've consecrated something that you will wear, such as a piece of jewelry or a robe, don't hesitate to put it on.

Herbs, Oils, and Crystals in Ritual and Celebration

RITUAL/ CELEBRATION	HERBS & OILS	CRYSTALS	COLORS
Samhain (Oct. 31)	Mugwort Rosemary Sage	Amber Hematite Obsidian	Black Orange Purple
Yule (Dec. 20–22)	Frankincense Holly Mistletoe	Garnet Green Tourmaline Ruby	Gold Green Red
Imbolc (Feb. 2)	Laurel Iris Myrrh Violet	Amethyst Bloodstone Moonstone	Red White
Ostara (Mar. 20–22)	Daffodil Lilac Willow	Agate Lapis Lazuli Rose Quartz	Lavender Pale Yellow Pastel Pink
Beltane (May 1)	Dogwood Lavender Thistle	Emerald Malachite Tourmaline	Bright Red Dark Green
Litha (June 20–22)	Basil Chamomile Lemon Balm Thyme	Amber Diamond Tiger's Eye Yellow Topaz	Orange Red Yellow
Lammas (Aug. 1)	Grains (Wheat, Corn) Grapevine Mint Sunflower	Citrine Moss Agate Obsidian	Light Brown Gold Tan
Mabon (Sept. 20–22)	Apple Blossom Cinnamon Marigold Sage	Carnelian Red Jasper	Burgundy Dark Red Deep Brown

RITUAL/ CELEBRATION	HERBS & OILS	CRYSTALS	COLORS
January/ Cold Moon	Birch Marjoram Thistle	Hematite Obsidian	Black Silver White
February/ Quickening Moon	Hyssop Myrrh Sage	Amethyst Jasper Rose Quartz	Blue Purple
March/ Storm Moon	Apple Blossom Pennyroyal	Aquamarine Bloodstone Turquoise	Lavender Light Blue Pastel Pink Pale Yellow
April/ Wind Moon	Dandelion Dill Milkweed	Quartz Selenite	Blue Green Red Yellow
May/ Flower Moon	Cinnamon Lavender Mint	Emerald Ruby	Green Red
June/ Strong Sun Moon	Basil Fern Moss	Agate Topaz	Orange Red Yellow
July/ Blessing Moon	Hyssop Mugwort Rue	White Agate Moonstone Opal Pearl	Pale Blue Silver White
August/ Corn Moon	Chamomile Rosemary Sunflower	Carnelian Red Agate Tiger's Eye	Orange Yellow

RITUAL/ CELEBRATION	HERBS & OILS	CRYSTALS	COLORS
September/ Harvest Moon	Valerian Wheat Witch Hazel	Bloodstone Citrine	Brown Gold Tan
October/ Blood Moon	Apple Blossom Squash Leaves Sweet Annie	Bloodstone Hematite Obsidian	Black Burgundy Dark Blue
November/ Mourning Moon	Betony Thistle	Lapis Lazuli Topaz	Blue Gray Silver
December/ Long Nights Moon	Holly Ivy Mistletoe	Topaz Turquoise	Black Red White

Herbs, Oils, and Crystals by Property and Purpose

PROPERTY/ PURPOSE/RITUAL	HERBS & OILS	CRYSTALS
Animal Magic	Catnip	Tiger's Eye
Banishing	Hyssop Lilac Pennyroyal Rue	Jet Obsidian Onyx
Calming	Basil Catnip Lavender	Emerald Quartz, Smoky Topaz, Blue
Cleansing & Purification	Catnip Chamomile Comfrey Hyssop Lavender Peppermint Sage Sandalwood Sweetgrass Tobacco	Amethyst Quartz, Clear Selenite
Divination & Spirit Communication	Basil Comfrey Dandelion Mugwort Tobacco	Selenite Turquoise
Dreams	Lavender	Obsidian
Fertility	Cinnamon Mistletoe Sunflower	Bloodstone Carnelian Shiva Lingam
Funerals & Death	Rosemary	Jet

PROPERTY/ PURPOSE/RITUAL	HERBS & OILS	CRYSTALS
Healing	Apple Blossom Comfrey Feverfew Hyssop Lavender Lemon Balm Mistletoe Peppermint Thistle Yarrow	Agate Amethyst Hematite Jasper Quartz, Clear Shiva Lingam Tiger's Eye
Intuition & Psychic Development	Cinnamon Mugwort Sage	Amethyst Diamond Garnet Hematite Moonstone Obsidian Quartz, Clear Turquoise
Love, Fidelity, Marriage	Apple Blossom Basil Catnip Cinnamon Lavender Lemon Balm Lilac Patchouli Peppermint Rosemary Sunflower Valerian Yarrow	Diamond Emerald Lodestone Quartz, Rose

PROPERTY/ PURPOSE/RITUAL	HERBS & OILS	CRYSTALS
Luck	Basil Catnip Chamomile Sunflower	Amethyst Carnelian Quartz, Rose
Lust	Mandrake Patchouli Yarrow	Carnelian Garnet Jasper
Meditation	Chamomile Sandalwood	Topaz
Money, Abundance, Prosperity	Apple Blossom Goldenseal Mandrake Patchouli Pennyroyal	Bloodstone Emerald Lodestone Topaz
Protection	Basil Comfrey Feverfew Holly Hyssop Mandrake Mistletoe Pennyroyal Rosemary Rue Thistle Tobacco Valerian	Amber Carnelian Hematite Onyx
Remembrance	Rosemary	Topaz, Pink

PROPERTY/ PURPOSE/RITUAL	HERBS & OILS	CRYSTALS
Strength, Confidence, Courage	Dandelion Holly Thistle Yarrow	Amber Hematite Onyx Tiger's Eye
Success & Power	Cinnamon Patchouli	Diamond Topaz, Yellow
Transformation & New Beginnings	Dandelion	Agate
Wisdom	Sage	Moonstone Turquoise
FOUR ELEMENTS/SUN & MOON		
Earth	Mugwort Patchouli	Agate Carnelian Jasper Jet Quartz, Clear Quartz, Smoky Shiva Lingam
Air	Dandelion Lavender Mistletoe Sage Sweetgrass	Diamond Quartz, Clear Shiva Lingam

PROPERTY/ PURPOSE/RITUAL	HERBS & OILS	CRYSTALS
Fire	Basil	Amber
	Cinnamon	Bloodstone
	Goldenseal	Diamond
	Holly	Hematite
	Hyssop	Obsidian
	Mandrake	Onyx
	Pennyroyal	Quartz, Clear
	Peppermint	Shiva Lingam
	Rosemary	Tiger's Eye
	Rue	Topaz
	Sunflower	
	Thistle	
	Tobacco	
Water	Apple Blossom	Amethyst
	Catnip	Lodestone
	Chamomile	Quartz, Clear
	Comfrey	Quartz, Rose
	Feverfew	Selenite
	Lemon Balm	Shiva Lingam
	Sandalwood	Turquoise
	Valerian	
	Yarrow	
Sun	Chamomile	Amber
	Mugwort	Topaz, Yellow
Moon	Mugwort	Moonstone
		Selenite

PROPERTY/ PURPOSE/RITUAL	HERBS & OILS	CRYSTALS
SABBATS		
Samhain	Comfrey Tobacco	Hematite Jet Obsidian Onyx
Yule	Cinnamon Holly Mistletoe	Bloodstone Jasper
Imbolc	Apple Blossom Lilac	Amethyst Bloodstone Garnet Onyx
Ostara	Dandelion Lilac	Agate Quartz
Beltane	Dandelion Lavender	Bloodstone Carnelian Shiva Lingam
Litha	Chamomile Lemon Balm Mistletoe Mugwort Sunflower Yarrow	Diamond Emerald Tiger's Eye
Lammas	Sage Sunflower	Amber Garnet
Mabon	Apple Blossom	Amethyst Hematite

PROPERTY/ PURPOSE/RITUAL	HERBS & OILS	CRYSTALS
SEASONS		
Fall	Apple Blossom Goldenseal Thistle	Hematite Obsidian Onyx
Winter	Cinnamon Holly Mistletoe	Bloodstone Garnet Jasper
Spring	Apple Blossom Lavender Lilac	Agate Amethyst Quartz
Summer	Chamomile Lemon Balm Mistletoe Sunflower	Amber Diamond Emerald

Your Book of Shadows

For most Wiccans today, the Book of Shadows, or BOS, is the corner-stone of magical practice. This is where you can store information on rituals, spells, herbal and crystal correspondences, prayers, deities, and anything else you might need along your journey to being an effective practitioner of magic. Like your athame or wand, the BOS is a magical tool and should be treated accordingly; it is sacred, an item of power.

Your Book of Shadows is a very personal thing, and just like you, it's unique. That means it should contain the information of the most value to you personally as you travel your spiritual journey.

Organizing Your Book of Shadows

To make your Book of Shadows, your best bet is to start with a blank notebook. You may prefer to use a three-ring binder so you can add and rearrange items later as needed. If you use a binder, you get the added benefit of being able to use clear plastic sheet protectors. You'll be glad you have them if you drip candle wax on your BOS during a ritual!

Your BOS can be handwritten if you like. Some people believe it's important to copy spells and rituals into the BOS by hand, because it transfers the spell's energy to the writer and also helps you memorize the contents. If you do a handwritten Book of Shadows, make sure you write legibly enough that can read your notes during a ritual! If you prefer not to handwrite your BOS, that's okay too; it's perfectly acceptable to use your computer to type up and print out information to put in your BOS.

Keep in mind that as technology changes, so does the way we use it. If you keep your entire BOS on a flash drive attached to your keychain, on your laptop, or even in cloud storage to be accessed with your smartphone, it's no less valid than one that is handwritten in ink on parchment.

The biggest issue most people run into with a Book of Shadows is how to keep it organized. It really is a matter of personal preference; you can use tabbed dividers, an index at the back, or even a table of contents in the front. The more you study and learn, the more information you'll want to include—and this is one reason why the three-ring binder method is popular.

No matter which method you choose, start off with a title page that includes your name and the date you began your BOS. It doesn't have to be elaborate; many Wiccans just write, *"The Book of Shadows of [Name]"* on the first page. You can also include a dedication if there's a specific goddess or god that you're going to dedicate yourself to.

When you find a ritual, spell, prayer, or other bit of information, be sure you note the source when you copy it into your BOS. You might even want to use one notebook or journal for information written by others and another for your original writings; this is a great way to inspire the creative spark!

Guidelines and Principles

Most people who follow a magical belief system have some sort of personal guidelines. You're the only one who can determine your own ethics and values, whether you follow the Wiccan Rede, the Rule of Three, or some other principle. Whatever it is that guides you, write it down in your BOS. This is a good philosophical exercise if you're just getting started; after all, if you write down what you believe to be acceptable magical behavior, it's always there as a reminder of personal boundaries later.

Deities and Prayers

Is there a specific goddess or god that you've connected to or that you'd like to learn more about? Be sure to log as much information about the deity as possible. Collect notes from a variety of sources, such as academic readings, mythology books, or websites. Go ahead and add images; while you can find plenty in books and online, this is a perfect opportunity to flex your creative muscle! Draw or paint your own visual representation of what the gods or goddesses look like to you. This is also a good place to keep prayers or songs you've found or composed in honor of the deities.

Correspondence Tables and Charts

Correspondence tables are the key to understanding magical theory. As we've discussed in this book, everything has its own unique magical signature. Keep notes on herbal and crystal correspondences, as well as colors, planets, wood, and even metals. Having these handy in a chart, where they're easily accessible, will make your spellcrafting a lot more efficient.

Rituals and Spells

If you're going to celebrate all eight of the Sabbats, as well as the moon phases each year, include rituals for each of these. For monthly Esbat rituals, you can use the same one each month, or you can create different ones for the various seasons. Include simple rituals that you know you'll be doing regularly, such as casting circles, god-honoring ceremonies, healing rites, or protection rituals.

Additional Material

The more you read, study, learn, and grow spiritually, the more information you're going to find. Add a section to your BOS that includes books and websites you've read or browsed through, and be sure to make notes on what you liked about them. If you didn't like them, write that down as well. You may even want to include sacred texts as you find them; even though Wicca itself isn't old, there is plenty of occult information out there, dating back hundreds of years.

You can also include information about basic methods of divination. If you've decided to start learning about reading Tarot cards, using a pendulum, or even astrology, write down exactly what you learn in each of your new practices.

When you're done creating your Book of Shadows, consecrate it and treat it as a sacred object.

GLOSSARY

Altar: a sacred place to perform spellwork, rituals, and other magical activities. The altar is typically the center of magic and ceremony for Wiccans.

Athame: a ceremonial knife used in Wiccan ritual for directing energy. It is typically not used for physical cutting but only for symbolic cutting.

Banishing: to get rid of or eliminate someone's influence or other negative aspects in your life by magical means.

Binding: to magically restrain someone from performing an action, such as harmful behaviors. In some cases, such as in handfastings, two people might voluntarily bind themselves together.

Boline: a curved, white-handled knife used in some Wiccan traditions for the harvesting of magical herbs.

Book of Shadows (BOS): a collection of spells, rituals, and other magical lore of use to Wiccans and other Pagans. The Book of Shadows is unique to each practitioner and is typically consecrated before use.

Cauldron: a vessel often made of cast iron and used for blending magical herbs, making offerings, burning incense, and many other magical purposes.

Censer: used to hold incense during ritual and ceremony.

Deosil: an archaic term found in many Wiccan traditions, meaning to move in a sunwise, or clockwise, direction. Deosil is associated with attraction and positivity.

Divination: to seek knowledge or awareness by metaphysical means. Many people use divination tools such as Tarot cards, pendulums, or astrology.

Element: the four elements, Earth, Air, Fire, and Water, that form the foundation of many Wiccan beliefs and practices.

Handfasting: a Pagan marriage ceremony, in which two people are physically and symbolically joined together with a cord wrapped around the wrists.

Neo-Wicca: forms of Wicca that are not the original traditions begun by Gerald Gardner and his initiates.

Offering: a gift or sacrifice presented to the gods, often as a way of saying thank you and expressing appreciation for the Divine.

Scrying: the practice of divination by staring into a reflective surface such as a mirror or water or even into flames in a fire.

Skyclad: the performance of ceremonies while nude, practiced by some Wiccans as a way of bringing themselves closer to the God and Goddess.

So mote it be: a phase often used at the conclusion of Wiccan spells and rituals as a way of designating that the speaker intends to manifest those spells and rituals.

Sympathetic magic: magic that uses symbolism to represent objects or actions. An example would be the use of healing magic on a doll representing an ill person.

Tradition: the core collection of beliefs and practices that defines one's spiritual system.

Widdershins: an archaic term found in some Wiccan traditions, meaning to move in a counterclockwise direction. Widdershins is associated with banishing and negativity.

Year and a day: historically used in Wicca to designate a study period. In many Wiccan traditions, new members are initiated after spending a year and a day studying and learning.

RESOURCES

Websites

Botanical.com This online herbal compendium contains extensive references on the medicinal and metaphysical properties of thousands of plants, and includes scientific knowledge as well as folklore.

Circlesanctuary.org One of the oldest Pagan nonprofit organizations in the world, Circle Sanctuary's website provides information on the basics of Wicca and other Pagan belief systems, as well as education and activism.

Pattiwigington.com Patti Wigington's main website.

Sarahannelawless.com A beautiful collection of information about sacred herbalism created by the author and artist Sarah Anne Lawless.

Themagickalcat.com This commercial website has a wide range of Wiccan products available, in addition to an extensive online grimoire with information on the magical properties of dozens of herbs and crystals.

Witchvox.com The Witches Voice is a comprehensive resource for Wiccans and other Pagans, containing links to educational articles, as well networking listings, sorted by location.

Books

Along with the books listed in the References section, consider adding the following titles to your reading list:

A Book of Pagan Prayer by Ceisiwr Serith (Weiser Books, 2002) Pagan prayers for every occasion and for a variety of Pagan belief systems, including Wicca. Follow some of the devotionals in this book to help strengthen your relationship with the Divine.

The Craft: A Witch's Book of Shadows by Dorothy Morrison (Llewellyn Publications, 2001) A detailed look at the basics of Wiccan practice, including spells, rituals, magical tool usage, and altar setup.

The Crystal Bible by Judy Hall (Walking Stick Press, 2003) Provides descriptions, full-color photos, and uses for hundreds of magical crystals and gemstones.

Cunningham's Encyclopedia of Magical Herbs by Scott Cunningham (Llewellyn Publications, 1985) A comprehensive list of hundreds of magical herbs, their properties, and uses.

Mixing Essential Oils for Magic: Aromatic Alchemy for Personal Blends by Sandra Kynes (Llewellyn Publications, 2013) A thorough look at the history and use of essential oils, from alchemy to modern magic. Includes step-by-step instructions for blending your own magical oil combinations.

Paganism: An Introduction to Earth-Centered Religions by River and Joyce Higginbotham (Llewellyn Publications, 2002) Takes a detailed look at the Divine and our connection to the gods by way of prayer, ritual, and how magic works, all presented in a balanced and straightforward way.

REFERENCES

Beyerl, Paul. *The Master Book of Herbalism*. Blaine, WA: Phoenix Publishing, 1984.

Campanelli, Pauline, and Dan Campanelli. *Wheel of the Year: Living the Magical Life*. 1st ed. Woodbury, MN: Llewellyn, 1989.

Cunningham, Scott. *The Complete Book of Incense, Oils, and Brews*. 1st ed. Woodbury, MN: Llewellyn, 1989.

Grieve, Margaret. *A Modern Herbal*. 2 vols. Mineola, NY: Dover Press, 1971.

Hall, Judy. *The Encyclopedia of Crystals*. Rev. ed. Gloucester, MA: Fair Winds Press, 2013.

Harrison, Karen. *The Herbal Alchemist's Handbook: A Grimoire of Philtres, Elixirs, Oils, Incense, and Formulas for Ritual Use*. Newburyport, MA: Weiser Books, 2011.

Melody. *Love Is in the Earth*. 3rd ed. Wheat Ridge, CO: Earth Love Publishing House, 1995.

Valiente, Doreen. *Witchcraft for Tomorrow*. London: Robert Hale, 1993.

Virtue, Doreen, and Judith Lukomski. *Crystal Therapy: How to Heal and Empower Your Life with Crystal Energy*. Carlsbad, CA: Hay House, 2005.

INDEX OF SPELLS

INDEX

ACKNOWLEDGMENTS

I'm fortunate enough to have been part of the Pagan community for my entire adult life, and I am remarkably blessed to know so many wonderful individuals, both online and in the mundane world. I'd like to thank the following amazing people for being a part of my life: LillyBeth Carman, Robin Smith, the entire Clan of the Stone Circle, Seamus Dillard and Leesa Kern, Terri Lynn Coop, Foinah Jameson, Sara Spock Carlson, my BoucherCon posse, Carole Oldroyd, Julie Fletcher, Nancy Basile, Amy Blackthorn, Byron Ballard, Angie Kunschmann, MJ Dellucci, and all the other incredible friends I've met along the way. Gratitude to every one of you for your love and support. You are magical, creative spirits, and I'm so glad you're part of my tribe.

ABOUT THE AUTHOR

PATTI WIGINGTON has been studying a variety of Pagan belief systems, including Wicca, since 1987. She is licensed Pagan clergy in Ohio and is the High Priestess and founder of Clan of the Stone Circle, a Celtic Pagan tradition. In 2007, Patti joined About.com as the Paganism/Wicca Expert. In addition to her work for About.com, Patti has written several novels and a children's book, and has contributed to numerous anthologies. She is the author of *The Good Witch's Daily Spell Book*, and you can find her online at pattiwigington.com.